quick-fix
vegan

healthy, homestyle
meals in

**30 minutes
or less**

quick-fix
vegan

robin robertson

**Andrews McMeel
Publishing, LLC**
Kansas City · Sydney · London

Andrews McMeel Publishing, LLC
an Andrews McMeel Universal company
1130 Walnut Street, Kansas City, Missouri 64106

www.andrewsmcmeel.com

11 12 13 14 15 RR2 10 9 8 7 6 5 4 3 2 1

ISBN: 978-1-4494-0-7858
Library of Congress Control Number: 2011921502

Photos by Ben Pieper, p. X, 84; all other photos courtesy of iStockphoto.com

www.globalvegankitchen.com

ATTENTION: SCHOOLS AND BUSINESSES
Andrews McMeel books are available at quantity discounts with bulk purchase
for educational, business, or sales promotional use. For information, please
e-mail the Andrews McMeel Publishing Special Sales Department:
specialsales@amuniversal.com

to all who extend the
circle of compassion
through a vegan lifestyle.

contents

acknowledgments

I'm fortunate to have a wonderful network of friends, family, and colleagues who enrich my life and my work. First and foremost I want to express my gratitude to a fantastic group of recipe testers: Jacqueline Bodnar, Jamie Coble, Lisa Dahlmeier, Linda Evans, Noelle Goveia, Mary Greenfield, Cassandra Greenwald, Lisa Harrington Seaman, Lea Jacobson, Kim Lahn, Ted Lai, Lori Maffei, Tami Noyes, Jenna Patton, Russell Patton, Eric Prescott, Kamber Sherrod, Elaine Trautwein, Andrea Weaver, Dianne Wenz, and Liz Wyman. Your enthusiasm for the recipes and your diligence in testing them made my job a dream.

Much love and gratitude to my husband and best friend Jon, for all you do. And to my cats Gary and Mitski, thanks for making me smile every day and for being excellent office cats.

I also want to thank the talented team at Andrews McMeel Publishing, especially my editor, Jean Lucas, as well as Diane Marsh, John Carroll, Dave Shaw, and Carol Coe. Thanks also to my agent, Stacey Glick of Dystel & Goderich Literary Management.

introduction

As much as I love to cook, most days I'm too busy to spend much time in the kitchen. That doesn't mean I skimp on healthy, well-balanced meals—I just figure out ways to save time and effort in preparing them.

As a plant-based diet becomes more mainstream, "vegan" has become the new "vegetarian." But even with more people realizing the many benefits of a plant-based diet, there remains a misconception that vegan cooking is time-consuming. With the recipes in this book, I hope to dispel that myth once and for all. By showing how quick and easy it is to get dinner on the table, "it takes too long" can no longer be an excuse not to cook vegan.

In my earlier book, *Quick-Fix Vegetarian*, I discussed how simple it is to prepare delicious plant-based meals by cooking smarter, not harder. Now, in *Quick-Fix Vegan*, I employ those same time-tested techniques, shortcuts, and strategies to bring you 150 delicious new plant-based recipes that can be prepared in 30 minutes or less.

With *Quick-Fix Vegan*, you can make healthy and economical meals even when there's little time to cook. From satisfying soups and salads such as Coconut Corn Chowder and Rainbow Rotini Salad to fabulous main dishes including Spicy Smoked Portobello Tacos and One-Pot Pasta Primavera, appetizers such as Bruschetta with Sicilian Greens and Easy Artichoke Puffs, and desserts like Chocolate Cheesecake Squares and Apple Pie Parfaits, these recipes will be the ones you'll rely on day in and day out.

Whether you're a new or longtime vegan, or just want to eat that way occasionally, *Quick-Fix Vegan* can be an invaluable resource to help you put healthy and delicious meals on the table with a minimum of time and effort.

quick-fix
vegan

getting started

The premise of this book is simple: quick and easy plant-based recipes that take 30 minutes or less of active preparation time. But there is more to it than that. Made with no animal products whatsoever, these recipes are also delicious and healthful, and designed to please everyone including vegetarians and omnivores. By virtue of the time constraint, the recipes are also inherently simple, making them ideal for the novice cook or those who simply don't have a lot of time to spend in the kitchen but still want to eat well.

Flexibility is another important factor in these recipes. I believe recipes, in general, are meant to be used as guidelines for creating particular dishes. For example, you may not like a particular ingredient in a recipe, or perhaps you don't have it on hand. The solution is simple: leave it out or substitute another ingredient for it, such as using parsley instead of cilantro. Seasoning is also very subjective. I've chosen the seasonings for these recipes in the hope that they will please most palates. However, every home cook should be in charge of their own seasonings, not just to make a recipe "their own," but to compensate for variables such as the relative flavors of certain ingredients, including the strength (and saltiness) of their vegetable broth, or the heat of the chiles they are using.

In this chapter, you'll find helpful information on the basics, including valuable advice on how to maintain a "quick-fix" vegan kitchen, a pantry list, kitchen tips, and equipment information. Recipes are also included for some basic ingredients used throughout the book, including vegetable broth and seitan for those who want to make them from scratch. Similar basic information can be found in my earlier book *Quick-Fix Vegetarian*, but the fundamental strategies are important to the quick-fix concept and bear repeating so you have them handy for making all new recipes in this book.

quick-fix vegan basics

If your busy schedule is keeping you out of the kitchen, then you've come to the right place. The recipes in this book can help you put a home-cooked meal on the table even when you're short on time.

One reason that quick-fix vegan recipes are important to me is that I want to dispel the notion that cooking vegan is especially time-consuming. With these recipes in hand, that tired old excuse goes right out the window. In the bargain, you'll not only be eating healthy, home-cooked meals, you'll be saving money too, since cooking vegan is also economical.

Basics discussed in this chapter include the elements that will help you have a quick-fix kitchen, including shopping tips, menu-planning, keeping a well-stocked pantry, and the judicious use of convenience foods.

time-saving strategies

Over the years, I've discovered lots of ways to save time in the kitchen, particularly when I worked as a restaurant chef and caterer. Here are some tips that I think you'll find indispensible:

- Wash and dry fresh produce when you bring it home from the market: This ensures that your ingredients are ready when you need them and allows you to remove any wilted leaves and so on. Exceptions to this strategy are mushrooms, berries, and other fragile ingredients that should only be washed immediately before using.
- Keep your kitchen well organized: This makes it easier, when you're ready to cook, to assemble your mise en place, which means gathering the ingredients and equipment you'll need. This includes

measuring out the ingredients in advance. If you do your mise en place prior to making each recipe, it will save you time and may also bump up the quality of your cooking to a higher level.

- Read and reread a recipe: When you are familiar with your recipe, and you have your ingredients and equipment at hand, you will be amazed at how much more easily you can prepare a meal. Good prep can also help avoid kitchen mishaps, such as missing ingredients, wrong pans, or burning up dinner while you search for a spice or a spatula.
- Be more intuitive or instinctive when you cook: By this I mean don't be afraid to substitute or change ingredients when it seems appropriate. For example, if you don't like a certain ingredient in a recipe, just make a reasonable substitution for something you do like, such as replacing tarragon with basil or pinto beans with kidney beans. In most cases, the recipe will turn out just as well and maybe better, since it will now have your own personal touch.
- Be flexible: While it's best to plan ahead and make sure in advance that you have everything you need in the house, it sometimes happens that you run out of an ingredient at the last minute. In those cases, rather than dropping everything to rush out to the store, try to determine if you have something in the house that can be substituted. To avoid running out of the ingredients you use most frequently, keep an ongoing grocery list in the kitchen so you can write down items the minute you run out or see that you're getting low.
- Keep a well-stocked pantry: The surest way to make certain you can get dinner on the table is to keep your pantry well supplied with the staples you most frequently use.

a quick-fix pantry

Keeping your pantry stocked with a good supply of your favorite ingredients means that a good meal can always be ready in minutes. Fact is, many delicious dishes can be made with convenient pantry ingredients. The wider the variety of ingredients you have, the more choices you will have at dinnertime.

on the pantry list

Here is a list of ingredients that can be used to create a variety of quick-and-easy meals. In addition to basics such as beans, whole grains, and pasta, I've included a variety of condiments, sauces, and other ingredients. Depending on your personal taste, consider keeping several of these ingredients on hand to add variety to your menus.

THE BASICS

Beans: Keep a variety of dried beans on hand to cook in large batches and then portion and freeze for ease of use. In addition to the dried beans, a supply of canned beans, such as chickpeas, kidney beans, cannellini beans, black beans, and pintos, can be the ultimate convenience foods on busy weeknights. Protein-rich beans are a great addition to pasta and grain dishes, as well as vegetable dishes and salads. Beans can be pureed for sauces, dips, and spreads, or mashed to make bean loaves, burgers, and more.

Grains: Some grains cook faster than others, such as quinoa and bulgur. Couscous and quick-cooking brown rice are also good to keep on hand. Longer-cooking grains can be made in large batches, portioned, and stored in the freezer for convenience.

Pasta: Keep a variety of pasta shapes on hand, including quick-cooking capellini, as well as orzo, thin rice noodles, and buckwheat soba.

Gnocchi and polenta: Look for shelf-stable vegan gnocchi that cook up in 3 minutes and can be used as a change from pasta, potatoes, or grains. Polenta is also available refrigerated in a log shape or in a shelf-stable rectangular shape and is great topped with chili or marinara sauce.

Flour tortillas, lavash, and other flatbreads: In addition to burritos, fajitas, and quesadillas, you can use tortillas and other flatbreads to make wrap sandwiches, layered casseroles, and even ultra-thin-crust pizzas.

Pizza dough: Buy ready-to-bake pizza dough to make quick and easy pizzas with your favorite toppings, or keep a stash of homemade pizza dough (see page 15) in the freezer.

Pie crust or dough: Frozen ready-to-use vegan pie crusts can come in handy. More economical is your own homemade pie dough (see page 16), individually wrapped and frozen. When ready to use, just thaw and roll out. Frozen vegan puff pastry—such as the Pepperidge Farm brand, which does not contain any animal ingredients—is also handy to keep in the freezer.

Vegetable broth: A world of choices awaits, from homemade broth portioned and frozen, to prepared broths in cans or aseptic containers. There is also a variety of vegetable broth pastes, powders, and cubes—just add water (see page 13).

Nondairy milk: There is a wide variety of nondairy milks now available including soy, rice, and almond milk. You can buy them in refrigerated cartons or aseptic containers. Many varieties come in different flavors including unsweetened (for savory recipes), as well as plain, vanilla, and chocolate.

Unsweetened coconut milk: Used in many Asian dishes, unsweetened coconut milk can also be used to enrich desserts, sauces, and other recipes.

- Tomato products: Canned tomatoes are practical and versatile and come in many forms including diced, whole, puree, paste.
- Bottled marinara sauce: Nothing beats the flavor of homemade marinara sauce, but keeping a jar of bottled sauce on hand can help you get a pasta meal on the table in minutes. Add a splash of red wine, fresh herbs, or sautéed mushrooms to give the sauce the taste of homemade.

BEYOND THE BASICS

For quick-fix cooking or for any cooking, for that matter, be sure to keep your pantry and/or refrigerator stocked with these additional items. You'll be glad you did.

Sun-dried tomatoes (dried or packed in oil)
Roasted red peppers
Tomato salsa
Dried chiles
Capers
Minced gingerroot (bottled)
Black or green olive tapenade
Black and green olives
Artichoke hearts (canned and frozen)
Miso paste
Vegan mayonnaise
Barbecue sauce
Hot chili paste
Sriracha sauce
Hoisin sauce
Soy sauce
Curry paste or powder
Chutney
Chipotle chiles in adobo
Peanut butter
Almond butter
Tahini (sesame paste)
Nutritional yeast
Nuts and seeds
Dried fruits: raisins, cranberries, apricots, etc.

ingredient shortcuts

Many recipes in this book call for ingredients that can be made either from scratch or purchased at the store. If you opt for store-bought, then all you need to do is stock your pantry. If you prefer to go the homemade route, then you need to keep a supply of those foods prepared and on hand.

Whether planning ahead means keeping containers of vegetable broth and beans in the freezer or buying canned vegetable broth and beans for the cupboard, the important thing is to keep essential ingredients on hand to prevent time-wasting extra shopping trips for one or two ingredients.

Without question, cooking beans and grains from scratch and making homemade broth are the best choices both nutritionally and economically. However, with today's hectic pace, cooking with canned beans and quick-cooking rice may be the only way some people can manage to cook healthy vegan meals. For that reason, the recipes in this book call for your choice of cooked or canned beans and often use quick-cooking grains. If you prefer to make certain ingredients from scratch, you'll save time if you plan ahead and portion and freeze ingredients such as beans and longer-cooking grains as described earlier in this chapter.

Since a 15-ounce can of beans usually contains about 1½ cups of beans, it's a good idea to portion and freeze your home-cooked beans in the same amounts. On average, 1 pound of dried beans will yield 4 to 6 cups cooked (depending on the bean), or the equivalent of 3 to 4 cans.

Other prepared ingredient shortcuts that can help save time are jarred roasted red peppers and bottled minced ginger. I also like to keep a bag of frozen bell pepper strips on hand for times when I need only a small amount of bell pepper for a recipe, when I've run out of fresh ones, or when the fresh bell peppers are too expensive.

Peeled garlic cloves, available in a jar in the produce section of the supermarket, are convenient time-savers, and they taste great. While minced garlic is also available in jars, I prefer the flavor quality of the whole peeled garlic cloves. A jar of peeled garlic cloves can also be a handy backup when the remains of your fresh garlic bulb have sprouted or dried up.

PREPARED VEGETABLE BROTH

If you prefer not to make homemade broth (see page 13), prepared vegetable broth available in cans and aseptic containers can be found at well-stocked supermarkets and natural food stores. The strength and flavor of the broth varies greatly by brand, so try one or two and decide which one you like best. In addition to these full-strength broths, you can buy vegan bouillon cubes, powdered vegetable base, and vegetable broth paste that become broth with the addition of boiling water.

Be aware that the saltiness of the different broths can vary widely (including your homemade batch). Many of the recipes in this book call for salt to be added "to taste." As stock reduces, saltiness increases, so you have to judge this carefully as you cook. As with any packaged food, check the ingredients for additives and buy the healthiest one (often the one with the fewest number of ingredients and the lowest amount of sodium). When using broths, initially taste them for strength, since some have stronger flavors that may encroach on the flavor of your finished dish. For a milder broth that is also more economical, dilute the canned broth by adding the equivalent amount of water. For example, if a recipe calls for 4 cups of broth, you can use 1 can of broth (approximately 2 cups) plus 2 cups of water.

A WORD ABOUT VEGETABLES

I'm an advocate of using as much locally grown, fresh organic produce as possible. However, I'm also realistic enough to realize that sometimes fresh organic produce is not available in the varieties we need, is astronomically priced, or is out of season. Also, if you limit your shopping to once per week, you may not be able to store enough fresh produce to last until your next shopping trip.

One solution can be to incorporate some frozen vegetables into your meals later in the week. Frozen veggies are already prepped and easy to use. Since they are frozen when they are fresh, they can be fresher than the "fresh" veggies in your supermarket, which may have been picked early and shipped long distances. Frozen vegetables are also economical, cook quickly, and can help you get through the week with quick and healthy meals.

Some frozen vegetables that find their way into my cooking include artichoke hearts, baby green peas, bell pepper strips, chopped spinach, corn kernels, and edamame. When fresh veggies aren't available, I also use some canned vegetables, especially tomatoes and tomato products, artichoke hearts, solid-pack pumpkin, and of course, canned beans of all kinds.

Even within the realm of fresh vegetables, there are convenience items that you can use to minimize prep time, including a wide variety of washed and prepared salad mixes from baby spinach to mixed field greens to crunchy romaine. Just open the bag and toss the leaves into a bowl. If you use a high-quality bottled vegan dressing, your salad is ready in seconds.

Also convenient are baby carrots, because they can be used without having to be peeled. Like bagged lettuces, bagged shredded cabbage is available, primarily for coleslaw, but it's also ideal when recipes call for shredded cabbage. For those in an unrelenting time crunch, you can save even more time by using presliced mushrooms, fresh chopped onions, and bags of fresh stir-fry vegetables.

Whenever you use precut vegetables or ready-to-eat salad greens, however, even those that are labeled "washed and ready to use," I recommend washing them again at home, just to be safe.

In the recipes in this book, it is assumed that vegetables are medium in size unless otherwise specified, and also that all fresh produce is washed, trimmed, and/or peeled before using, unless otherwise specified.

NONDAIRY MILK

Nondairy milk, including those made from soy, almonds, rice, and oats, can be used in recipes in the same way dairy milk is used. For savory recipes, it's important to use unsweetened varieties, however, since some brands of nondairy milk contain added sugar, even those labeled "plain."

Other nondairy products such as vegan versions of mayonnaise, butter, cheese, cream cheese, sour cream, and yogurt can be used instead of dairy products in recipes as well.

TOFU, TEMPEH, AND SEITAN

Protein-rich foods such as tempeh, tofu, and seitan are popular plant-based alternatives to meat. In addition to these mainstays, prepared vegan protein options include burgers, sausages, and burger "crumbles." These products can be used to replace meat in recipes that normally call for meat, or they can be enjoyed in interesting new ways.

While tofu and tempeh are widely available and reasonably priced, buying prepared seitan can be expensive and may be harder to find in some regions. In addition, the flavor of commercially prepared seitan can vary by brand, and depending on how it is seasoned, that flavor might interfere with your recipe. Homemade seitan, on the other hand, is simple and economical to make. On page 14, you will find a basic seitan recipe that can be made three different ways: on top of the stove, in the oven, or in a slow cooker. You can also vary the seasonings according to taste. Once cooled, seitan can be wrapped and refrigerated or frozen to use in recipes.

OTHER INGREDIENTS

In an effort to make this book user-friendly, I've done my best to use easy-to-find ingredients in the recipes. I don't want you to avoid a recipe simply because you can't find a particular ingredient. At the same time, if you have personal preferences, feel free to substitute ingredients you like for ones that you don't. For example, if you don't enjoy the kidney beans called for in a recipe, but you love chickpeas, go ahead and use the chickpeas instead. As mentioned earlier, this applies to seasonings as well. If you prefer more or less of certain seasonings, feel free to season foods according to your own taste. Similarly, for lower-fat recipes, simply use vegetable broth or nonstick spray for sautéing, instead of using oil.

You may notice that some recipes call for hard vegetables such as carrots that are thinly sliced, finely chopped, or shredded. This is because the thinner a vegetable is sliced, the quicker it will cook.

When olive oil is listed in a recipe, it refers to extra-virgin olive oil. When salt is listed, sea salt is preferred. When chopped scallions are listed, it refers to both the white and green parts. For sugar, I prefer an organic natural sugar rather than the highly processed white table sugar.

When specific can or jar sizes are called for, these sizes are based on what is available in my local store. If your store carries 16-ounce canned beans and the recipe calls for a 15-ounce can, go with the size found in your store. Such a small difference in size won't affect the recipe results.

plan ahead

The best way to ensure that you can get dinner on the table in 30 minutes or less involves some advance planning in the form of an ongoing grocery list and a menu plan for the week. Here are some ways to incorporate list making into your routine:

Keep a list of your family's favorite dishes and rotate them regularly.

Plan meals in advance, serving make-ahead one-dish meals on especially busy nights.

Plan your menus: This doesn't have to be a complete formal menu plan. Instead, just make a brief note such as: "Monday: chili; Tuesday: tempeh stir-fry; Wednesday: pasta and salad;" and so on. Having an idea of your menus for the week will help you with your grocery shopping and save you time all week long. Refer to your notes when you make your grocery list so you'll have all your ingredients on hand.

Make a master grocery list once and photocopy it for future use.

Keep your grocery list handy to jot items on the list as they become low.

Organize your pantry shelves so you know where everything is at a glance.

Keep a variety of condiments on hand that add flavor to a recipe. I especially favor soy sauce, sriracha sauce, chutney, and salsa.

Save time at the supermarket by being familiar with the store layout (many grocery stores have maps) and write your grocery list in the same order as you'll trek the store aisles.

Take advantage of sales and have some flexibility regarding ingredient choices. For example, when the store has a sale on asparagus, you want to buy extra to enjoy before the price goes back up.

QUICK-FIX COOK-A-THONS

When time is at a premium, consider doing a weekly cook-a-thon during which you prepare several meals at once. Set aside a few hours to spend in the kitchen—I usually schedule mine on Sunday afternoons, when I put on some music and prepare a few dishes to get me through the week. I like to prepare things that reheat well or that can be portioned and frozen, such as a pot of chili, a hearty soup, a casserole, or a grain pilaf. It's also a great time to cook a big batch of brown rice, dried beans, or vegetable broth to portion and freeze.

Here are some guidelines for cook-a-thons:

Prepare double batches of long-cooking recipes, such as stews, soups, and chili. Bonus: Their flavor improves when reheated, so they're even better when served later in the week or after being frozen for a time.

Cook a large pot of a staple grain or bean—I usually make a different kind of bean each week, so I can have a variety portioned and frozen for later use. When you need them, just thaw and heat.

Double up on prep work, such as chopping onions, when making more than one recipe, so you have enough for all of them. When you need only half an onion, chop the whole onion and refrigerate the unused portion in a sealed bag.

Wash lettuces and other vegetables when you bring them home from the store. This will save you time when you want to make a quick meal.

LOVE THOSE LEFTOVERS

I love leftovers, and not just those soups or stews that taste even better reheated. I even enjoy the solitary leftover baked potato or that small amount of vegetables that were overlooked last night at dinner. Leftovers are fun to transform into a second meal that is entirely different from the first way it was served. This not only helps if you have family members who don't like to eat the same thing two days in a row, it's also economical, since it can help stretch your food dollar and eliminate waste. With a little ingenuity, there are lots of creative ways to use leftovers.

For example, that leftover potato can be diced or sliced and sautéed with chopped onions, oregano, and lemon juice for a terrific side dish of Greek-style potatoes. You could also mash it up with some leftover vegetables and make fritters or even a stuffing for samosas.

I sometimes even make dinner with a second meal in mind. Chili is a prime example. You can enjoy the chili "as is" one day and then use the leftovers to make a layered Mexican-style casserole with soft tortillas, salsa, and other ingredients. Spoon leftover stew into a casserole dish, top with a ready-to-use pie crust, and pop it into the oven for a quick and easy potpie. Puree a small amount of leftover vegetable soup to use in a flavorful primavera sauce for pasta. Just as leftover vegetables can be used in a quiche or casserole, or added to composed salads or pasta and grain dishes, so too can a small amount of leftover pasta, potatoes, or rice be added to salads or soups for a hearty main dish meal.

Begin to think about preparing food that can be incorporated into another meal. For example, if you need only half a box of pasta for a meal, cook the entire box anyway. Toss what you don't use with a small amount of olive oil, cover, and refrigerate until needed.

Having extra cooked pasta on hand can save time when making dinner another night, using the pasta in a different way.

HOMEMADE CONVENIENCE FOODS

Ready-made food from the supermarket can save time when preparing a meal. The downside to that convenience is the added expense. You can make many such convenience foods, such as broth and pizza dough, at home in quantity, and then portion and freeze them. One of the most economical items to make from scratch is vegetable broth. A recipe for homemade broth, as well as other homemade convenience foods, including seitan, pie dough, and pizza dough, can be found on pages 13 to 17.

kitchen equipment

While good kitchen equipment is important, I believe that cooking is more about the cook and the quality of the ingredients. Buy the best quality equipment you can afford, but you don't necessarily need to have a huge set of pots and pans (or other equipment) when just a few will do.

Every kitchen needs at least one pot big enough to boil pasta and make several quarts of vegetable broth. You also need a couple of smaller saucepans, including one with a steamer insert for steaming vegetables. Two or three heavy-bottomed skillets, ranging in size from 8 to 16 inches in diameter, are a must. At least one skillet should have a nonstick surface. All pots and skillets should have lids that fit well. When the term "skillet" appears in recipes, it means "medium-size" (10 to 12-inch) unless otherwise indicated.

Other kitchen basics include a few mixing bowls, a set of measuring cups and spoons, a colander, cutting boards, and baking dishes and pans. Nothing much beyond these is required to make the recipes in this book. In addition, there are a few kitchen tools that can help make cooking faster and easier:

Knives: There are three knives that no kitchen should be without: a paring knife for peeling and trimming; a long serrated knife for slicing bread, tomatoes, and other fragile foods; and a good (8 or 10-inch) chef's knife for virtually everything else. Buy the best quality knives you can afford and keep them sharp. You can chop more quickly and safely with sharp knives than dull ones.

Food processor: A food processor is essential for making pesto, pureeing vegetables, chopping nuts, and making bread crumbs. It is also great for making pie dough, chopping vegetables, and numerous other mixing and chopping tasks. The trick is knowing when it will be faster to cut, whisk, or chop by hand, and that can usually be determined by the quantity of food involved. In addition to a large-capacity processor, some people also have a smaller model that they use for smaller tasks.

Blender: For the longest time, I got along with just a food processor and no blender at all. Then I acquired a high-powered blender (Vitamix) and my cooking habits changed. I now use both blender and food processor for different purposes. The blender is reserved for smoothies, sauces, soups, and anything I want to make supersmooth and creamy very quickly. Another plus of having both a food processor and a blender in play is that I can often avoid stopping to wash out one or the other when making multiple recipes.

Immersion blender: The advantage to the immersion blender is that it is easier to clean than the regular blender and it saves the time it takes to pour your recipe into a blender container, since you can blend the food right in the bowl. It's especially handy for pureeing soup right in the cooking pot.

Box grater: This versatile tool can be used when you have a small amount of food that needs grating or shredding (instead of dirtying the food processor). It works well for anything from citrus zest to cabbage. For small jobs, use a rasp grater (such as a Microplane).

Mandoline: I use a mandoline when I need very thin slices very fast. Sure, you can always slice ingredients with a knife or even the slicing attachment of a food processor, but this handy gadget lets you cut uniform slices, from thick to paper-thin, with ease and swiftness—just watch your fingers because the blades are very sharp. Note: The plastic Benriner slicer is a smaller version of the stainless-steel mandoline and is much less expensive, making it a good choice if you're on a budget.

Salad spinner: Spinning your salad greens is the easiest and quickest way to dry them after washing. It gets every drop of water off your lettuce, leaving it crisp and ready for your salad.

Vegetable peeler: Indispensable for peeling carrots, potatoes, cucumbers, and the like, a peeler is quick, easy, and very low-tech.

Microwave: While I would never actually cook dinner in a microwave, it can be a useful tool to help get dinner on the table. It's ideal when you need a small amount of melted vegan butter, chocolate, or hot liquid. You can use it to soften hard winter squashes to make them easier to cut. It's also a convenient way to reheat leftovers.

basic recipes: convenience foods from scratch

One of the key points to getting dinner on the table in 30 minutes or less is having all the ingredients you need at the ready. Some ingredients are naturally quick cooking, while others need to be made ahead or purchased ready-made at the store. A few of these basic "convenience" foods are easy and economical to make from scratch. Here are the recipes and cooking instructions for some of the items frequently called for in my recipes. I've also included descriptions of the store-bought versions of these ingredients that can be found at well-stocked supermarkets and natural food stores.

In addition, you will find instructions on how to toast nuts and roast bell peppers, both of which can also be bought prepared but are easy to make at home.

vegetable broth

makes about 2 quarts

This basic vegetable broth can be cooled and frozen in several storage containers with tight-fitting lids so you can defrost exactly what you need for a recipe. Be sure to scrub and wash all vegetables well before using. For information on commercial vegetable broths, vegan bouillon cubes, and powdered vegetable base, see page 7.

1 tablespoon olive oil
1 large yellow onion, coarsely chopped
2 large carrots, coarsely chopped
1 large russet potato, unpeeled and cut into chunks
2 celery ribs, including leaves, coarsely chopped

3 cloves garlic, crushed
3 quarts water
2 tablespoons soy sauce
1 cup coarsely chopped fresh parsley
2 bay leaves
½ teaspoon salt
½ teaspoon black peppercorns

Heat the oil in a large stockpot over medium heat. Add the onion, carrots, potato, celery, and garlic. Cover and cook until slightly softened, about 5 minutes. Add the water, soy sauce, parsley, bay leaves, salt, and peppercorns. Bring to a boil, then reduce the heat to medium-low and simmer, uncovered, to reduce the liquid and bring out the flavors of the vegetables, 1 hour.

Strain the liquid through a fine-mesh sieve into another pot, pressing the juices out of the vegetables with the back of a large spoon. The broth is now ready to use. For a stronger broth, bring the broth back to a boil, and reduce the volume by one-quarter. This broth keeps well in the refrigerator for up to 3 days if kept tightly covered, or portioned and frozen for up to 4 months.

seitan three ways

makes about 2 pounds

This is my go-to seitan recipe. It makes about 2 pounds that can be portioned into 8-ounce packages and frozen for later use. It can also be stored in the refrigerator for up to 3 days either in a covered container in its cooking broth or portioned and tight-wrapped. I've included cooking instructions to make it 3 different ways: on top of the stove, in the oven, or in a slow cooker. This seitan can be used in any of the recipes in this book that call for seitan.

2 cups vital wheat gluten flour
¼ cup nutritional yeast
3 tablespoons tapioca flour
1 teaspoon garlic powder
1 teaspoon onion powder
½ teaspoon salt

¼ teaspoon freshly ground black pepper
1½ cups cold water
2 tablespoons soy sauce
2 tablespoons olive oil
4 cups cold vegetable broth (for stovetop and slow cooker methods)

In a food processor or bowl, combine the vital wheat gluten flour, nutritional yeast, tapioca flour, garlic powder, onion powder, salt, and pepper and pulse or stir to mix. Add the water, soy sauce, and oil, and process or stir to mix well. Turn the mixture out onto a flat surface and knead into a cohesive dough, 2 minutes. Let the dough rest for 5 minutes.

Stovetop: Divide the dough into 4 equal pieces and place them in a large pot with enough cold vegetable broth to cover. Bring almost to a boil, then reduce the heat to a simmer and cook for 1 hour. Let the seitan cool to room temperature in the broth.

Slow Cooker: Divide the dough into 4 equal pieces and place them in a slow cooker with enough vegetable broth to cover. Cook on low for 8 hours. Cool to room temperature in the slow cooker.

Bake: Preheat the oven to 350°F. Flatten the seitan into a 6-inch square and enclose it loosely in a sheet of aluminum foil. Place the seitan packet in a shallow baking dish and add enough water to come halfway up the seitan packet. Cover the baking pan tightly with foil and bake until firm, 1 hour. Remove the seitan from the pan, remove the foil, and set aside to cool to room temperature.

For all three methods, once the seitan has cooled to room temperature, it is ready to use in recipes. For the best texture, the seitan should be refrigerated for at least an hour to firm up before using. It can be refrigerated either in the broth in a covered container or removed from the broth and tightly wrapped. The seitan will keep well in the refrigerator for 3 days or in the freezer for up to 3 months, when tightly wrapped and frozen.

pizza dough

makes dough for 2 (12-inch) pizzas

I like to make enough dough for 2 pizzas at a time (even when I need only one). That way I can stash the extra one in the freezer for a future meal. I find it quicker to make the dough in a food processor, but you can make it in a stand mixer or in a bowl by hand, if you prefer. For extra flavor, add 1 teaspoon garlic powder or 1 teaspoon dried Italian seasoning to the dough. If not using right away, the dough can be tightly wrapped and frozen for 2 to 3 months, then thawed in the refrigerator and brought to room temperature before shaping into a crust and baking.

3 cups unbleached all-purpose flour
2¼ teaspoons instant-rise yeast
1¼ teaspoons salt

½ teaspoon sugar
1½ tablespoons olive oil
1 cup warm water

Lightly oil the inside of a large bowl and set aside. In a food processor (or using a stand mixer), combine the flour, yeast, salt, and sugar. With the machine running, add the oil through the feed tube and slowly add the water as needed until a slightly sticky dough ball forms.

Transfer the dough to a floured surface and knead until it is smooth and elastic, 1 to 2 minutes. Shape the dough into a smooth ball and place it in the prepared bowl. Turn the dough to coat it with oil, then cover the bowl with plastic wrap and let the dough rise at room temperature in a warm area until doubled in size, about 1 hour.

Punch down the dough and divide it into 2 pieces. On a lightly floured surface, shape each piece into a round ball. Cover and let it rest for about 30 minutes. The dough is now ready to use in recipes.

To bake a pizza, preheat the oven to 450°F. Turn the dough onto a floured surface and shape to fit your pizza pan, add toppings of choice, and bake for about 10 minutes. You can use this dough to make the pizza recipes on pages 160 and 161.

pie dough

makes enough for 2 crusts

This recipe makes enough for 1 double-crust pie or 2 single-crust pies. Make ahead and freeze the flattened dough for when you need it. Then simply defrost and roll out the dough.

2 cups unbleached all-purpose flour
1 teaspoon salt
2/3 cup vegan butter, cut into small pieces
   (try Earth Balance brand)
4 tablespoons ice water, or more if needed

Combine the flour and salt in a food processor. Blend in the vegan butter with short pulses, until the mixture becomes crumbly. With the machine running, add water through the feed tube and pulse until the dough just starts to hold together. Transfer the dough to a work surface, divide it in half, and flatten to form two disks. Wrap the dough in plastic wrap and refrigerate for 30 minutes before rolling out. If you refrigerate the dough until it's stiff, let it sit out until it's pliable enough to roll, about 15 minutes.

note: Frozen pie crusts (in aluminum pie plates) are available in supermarkets and natural food stores. Be sure to read the label carefully since some brands may contain lard or butter.

roasted bell peppers

Here's an easy way to roast bell peppers: Preheat the broiler. Cut the peppers in half lengthwise, and remove the stems, seeds, and membranes. Cut 1-inch slits at the edges as necessary so the peppers lie flat. Arrange the pepper halves on a foil-lined baking sheet, and place under the broiler until the skin is blistered and blackened. Set aside to cool. With this method, you can roast several peppers at once and they're under the broiler just a few minutes. You don't have to stand at a flame or grill, rotating the pepper, doing one at a time. Then, simply peel them when they're cool enough to handle.

note: Bottled roasted red peppers are sold in supermarkets in 6-ounce and 12-ounce jars, packed in oil.

toasted nuts

Nuts can be toasted in 2 ways—either on top of the stove in a dry skillet, or in the oven on a baking sheet.

To toast nuts in the oven, preheat the oven to 350°F. Place the nuts in a single layer in a small shallow baking pan. Toast until very lightly browned and fragrant, stirring occasionally, 2 to 8 minutes, depending on the type of nut. Pine nuts, sliced almonds, and sesame seeds, for example, begin to brown very quickly, while heartier nuts such as walnuts and pecans take longer. Remove toasted nuts from the oven and cool completely.

To toast nuts on the stovetop, place them in a dry small skillet over medium heat and toast them, stirring or shaking the pan occasionally, until lightly browned, 1 to 5 minutes, depending on the nut. Be careful not to burn them. Cool completely.

note: For convenience, some varieties of nuts are sold already toasted.

about the recipes

One of my goals in this book has been to develop recipes that take no longer than 30 minutes of active time to prepare. By "active" time, I mean the actual hands-on time it takes to prepare the recipe. It does not include the time it takes to gather your equipment and ingredients together or wash your produce. The recipes in *Easy Make-Ahead Bakes* also adhere to less than 30 minutes of active time, but that doesn't include the in-oven baking time. Those oven-baked recipes are especially convenient because they can be assembled ahead of time and then baked when you're ready to eat them. Plus, since you bake and serve right in the same baking dish, there's no messy cleanup to worry about. In terms of convenience and variety, recipes that can be assembled ahead of time can be the quickest meals to fix.

From lightening-quick appetizers and main dishes, to speedy soups, sandwiches, salads, and desserts, I hope you enjoy preparing the recipes in *Quick-Fix Vegan* as much as I enjoyed creating them.

chapter 2

starters and snacks

Because appetizers or hors d'oeuvres are often thought to be time-consuming and fussy, I called this chapter "Starters and Snacks" to highlight the quick and casual nature of these recipes. Not just for parties or get-togethers, although they're ideal for those occasions, too, these versatile recipes are great anytime. For example, Hummamole (a delicious fusion of hummus and guacamole) is fantastic as a spread for sandwiches and wraps. The Chickpea and Spinach–Artichoke Crostini makes a great lunch on its own, and the Vegetable Fritters, Provençal Stuffed Mushrooms, and Bruschetta with Sicilian Greens can also be enjoyed as light suppers when accompanied by a green salad or a bowl of soup.

From tasty spreads and dips to flaky pastry bites, these recipes are amazingly quick and easy to prepare and are so packed with flavor, they taste like they took all day to make.

moroccan pumpkin hummus

makes about 2 cups

This colorful and spice-happy take on hummus will turn heads and wake up taste buds at your next gathering. If you prefer great flavor without the heat, just leave out the cayenne. Serve with pita chips.

1 tablespoon olive oil
2 cloves garlic, chopped
1 teaspoon ground ginger
1 teaspoon ground coriander
¼ teaspoon ground cinnamon
¼ teaspoon ground allspice
½ teaspoon ground turmeric
⅛ teaspoon cayenne
¼ teaspoon sugar

2 tablespoons tahini
1 cup home-cooked or canned chickpeas
1 cup canned pumpkin puree
2 tablespoons freshly squeezed lemon juice
½ teaspoon salt
¼ teaspoon freshly ground black pepper
1 tablespoon chopped pistachios, for garnish

Heat the oil in a skillet over medium heat. Add the garlic, ginger, coriander, cinnamon, allspice, turmeric, cayenne, and sugar and cook until fragrant, 1 to 2 minutes. Stir in the tahini and chickpeas, then remove from the heat. Stir in the pumpkin, lemon juice, salt, and pepper. Transfer the mixture to a food processor and process until smooth. Transfer to a shallow serving bowl and sprinkle the pistachios on top. Serve immediately, or cover and refrigerate until needed.

spicy black bean hummus with orange

makes about 1½ cups

Creamy black beans and hot chiles merge deliciously with the bright flavor of orange in this tasty and exotic hummus. Pita chips, or other sturdy chips, make an ideal accompaniment.

1 to 2 jalapeño or serrano chiles, seeded and chopped

2 cloves garlic, chopped

½ teaspoon salt

1½ cups home-cooked black beans, or 1 (15-ounce) can, drained and rinsed

3 tablespoons freshly squeezed orange juice

2 tablespoons sesame tahini

1 teaspoon finely grated orange zest

½ teaspoon ground cumin

2 tablespoons minced fresh parsley or cilantro

Combine the chiles, garlic, and salt in a food processor and process until finely minced. Add the beans, orange juice, tahini, orange zest, and cumin, and process until smooth, scraping down the bowl as needed. Taste and adjust the seasonings.

Transfer to a small bowl. Sprinkle the parsley on top of the hummus and around the edge of the bowl. Serve at once or cover and refrigerate until needed.

hummamole

makes about 2½ cups

Easy, delicious, and lower in fat and higher in protein than regular guacamole, this hummus-guacamole hybrid is also just a bit different from your average hummus. I considered calling it "guacmus," but I think "hummamole" has a nicer ring to it, don't you? In addition to making a great dip for chips or raw veggies, it also makes a yummy spread for wrap sandwiches.

1 ripe avocado
1½ cups home-cooked chickpeas,
   or 1 (15-ounce) can, drained and rinsed
2 cloves garlic, crushed
1 tablespoon tahini
1 tablespoon freshly squeezed lemon juice

½ teaspoon ground cumin
¼ teaspoon salt
Pinch of cayenne
1 tablespoon chopped fresh cilantro, for
   garnish

Halve and pit the avocado, spoon out the flesh, and place it in a food processor. Add the chickpeas, garlic, tahini, 1 tablespoon lemon juice or to taste, the cumin, salt, and cayenne and process until smooth. Taste and adjust the seasonings. If a thinner consistency is desired, blend in up to 2 tablespoons of water. Transfer to a bowl and sprinkle with the cilantro. Serve at once or cover and chill until needed.

smokin' guacamole

serves 6

The smoky heat of the chipotles is the secret ingredient in this flavorful guacamole. One taste and the delicious secret will be out. Serve with tortilla chips.

2 ripe Hass avocados
2 tablespoons freshly squeezed lemon or
   lime juice
1 ripe Roma tomato, minced

1 clove garlic, minced
3 tablespoons minced scallions
2 canned chipotle chiles in adobo, minced
¼ teaspoon salt

Halve and pit the avocados, spoon out the flesh, and transfer to a bowl. Add the lemon juice and mash well. Add the tomato, garlic, scallions, chiles, and salt and mix well to combine. Serve at once or cover and refrigerate until needed.

red bean–chipotle dip

serves 6

This boldly flavored dip is wonderful paired with crunchy tortilla chips. It can also double as a spread in wrap sandwiches. For a less spicy dip, use only 1 chipotle.

1½ cups home-cooked dark red kidney
   beans, or 1 (15-ounce) can, drained
   and rinsed
2 chipotle chiles in adobo
¼ cup chopped scallions
1 clove garlic, chopped

½ teaspoon salt
¼ teaspoon ground cumin
1 tablespoon freshly squeezed lime juice
¼ cup water
Minced scallions, or fresh parsley or
   cilantro, for garnish

Combine the beans, chiles, chopped scallions, garlic, salt, cumin, lime juice, and water in a food processor and pulse until well blended. Transfer to a bowl. Garnish and serve at once, or cover and refrigerate until needed, then garnish and serve.

artichoke and bell pepper tapenade on toast

serves 6

Bold Mediterranean flavors combine in one zesty tapenade. Served here on bite-size pieces of toast, it can also be used as a topping for crostini or bruschetta or a filling for stuffed cherry tomatoes. Instructions for roasting your own bell peppers are on page 16.

1 large roasted red bell pepper (see page 16), or 1 (6-ounce) jar, well drained and blotted dry
1 (6-ounce) jar marinated artichoke hearts, well drained and blotted dry
¼ cup pitted kalamata olives, halved

2 tablespoons oil-packed sun-dried tomatoes, blotted dry
2 tablespoons capers, drained
Salt and freshly ground black pepper
6 to 8 slices firm bread

Preheat the oven to 400°F. In a food processor, combine the bell pepper, artichoke hearts, olives, sun-dried tomatoes, capers, and salt and pepper to taste. Pulse until well combined and finely minced, but not pureed. Transfer to a bowl and set aside.

Use a knife or pastry cutter to cut the bread into bite-size shapes and arrange in a single layer on baking sheets. Bake until toasted on both sides, turning once, about 10 minutes total. Or, you can toast the bread slices in a toaster and then cut them afterward. To serve, spread the tapenade onto the toasted bread and serve immediately.

chickpea and spinach–artichoke crostini

serves 6

Made with a few pantry ingredients, this terrific appetizer takes only minutes to prepare. The creamy and piquant topping, made with chickpeas, artichokes, and sun-dried tomatoes, is positively addictive served on toasted ciabatta bread slices. In addition to crostini, the topping can also be spread onto wrap sandwiches or served as a dip with crackers.

2 to 3 cloves garlic, crushed
2 cups packed baby spinach or arugula
1½ cups home-cooked chickpeas, or
   1 (15-ounce) can, drained and rinsed
1 (6-ounce) jar marinated artichoke hearts,
   drained
¼ cup oil-packed sun-dried tomatoes,
   drained and chopped
¼ cup coarsely chopped fresh basil

2 tablespoons freshly squeezed lemon juice
1 tablespoon olive oil
¼ teaspoon salt
⅛ teaspoon freshly ground black pepper
1 loaf ciabatta bread, cut into ½-inch thick
   slices
Ground fennel seed (optional)
1 basil sprig, for garnish

Preheat the oven to 400°F. In a food processor, mince the garlic with the spinach. Add the chickpeas, artichokes, tomatoes, basil, lemon juice, oil, salt, and pepper. Process until almost smooth. Add up to 2 tablespoons of water if the mixture seems dry, then pulse to combine. Taste and adjust the seasoning.

Arrange the bread slices in a single layer on a baking sheet. Bake until golden brown, about 5 minutes.

Serve at room temperature, or warm to bring out the flavors. To warm the topping, microwave for 1 minute or heat in a small saucepan over low heat, then transfer to a bowl. When ready to serve, sprinkle with fennel, if using, and top with the sprig of basil. Spread the topping onto the toasted bread and serve.

bruschetta with sicilian greens

serves 6

Typically Sicilian, toasted bread is topped with dark greens sautéed in olive oil and garlic with crunchy walnuts and sweet raisins. Capers and the optional red pepper flakes provide additional flavor notes.

6 cups packed fresh spinach or chard
3 cloves garlic
½ cup walnut pieces
3 tablespoons golden raisins
2 tablespoons capers

¼ teaspoon red pepper flakes (optional)
1 tablespoon olive oil
Salt and freshly ground black pepper
1 baguette, cut diagonally into ½-inch
   slices

Preheat the oven to 400°F. In a food processor, combine the spinach, garlic, walnuts, raisins, capers, and red pepper flakes, if using. Heat the oil in a skillet over medium heat. Add the spinach spread and season to taste with salt and pepper. Cook, stirring, until the spinach is wilted and the garlic is fragrant, about 3 minutes. Keep warm while you toast the bread.

Arrange the bread slices in a single layer on a baking sheet. Bake until golden brown, about 5 minutes. To serve, transfer the spinach mixture to a bowl and serve warm spooned onto the toasted bread.

two-tomato pastry purses

makes 16

Frozen vegan puff pastry is my secret weapon for easy quick-fix entertaining. Here, sweet cherry tomatoes and sun-dried tomatoes team up for a luscious filling in these flaky pastry purses.

2 teaspoons olive oil
3 cloves garlic, minced
2 scallions, minced
2 cups cherry tomatoes, chopped
¼ cup oil-packed sun-dried tomatoes, minced

3 tablespoons chopped kalamata olives
2 tablespoons minced fresh basil
Salt and freshly ground black pepper
1 sheet frozen vegan puff pastry, thawed

Preheat the oven to 400°F. Heat the oil in a skillet over medium heat. Add the garlic and scallions and cook until fragrant, 30 seconds. Add the cherry tomatoes, sun-dried tomatoes, olives, and basil. Season to taste with salt and pepper. Cook, stirring, until the tomatoes release their liquid, a few minutes. Transfer to a bowl and refrigerate.

Roll out the pastry on a flat surface and cut into 16 equal squares. Drain off any watery liquid from the tomato mixture. Place a teaspoonful of the tomato mixture in the center of a pastry square. Gather the four corners of the pastry and bring them to the center, pressing together to seal the filling inside the "purse." Repeat with the remaining filling and pastry. Arrange the filled pastry purses on an ungreased baking sheet. Bake until golden brown, about 18 minutes. Serve warm.

curried puff pastry nibbles

serves 8

Almost effortless to make, these flavorful nibbles make great party fare. They're also quite delicious served with an Indian meal.

2 tablespoons finely crushed roasted
   unsalted cashews (see note)
1 tablespoon mild or hot curry powder
½ teaspoon ground coriander

½ teaspoon ground cumin
½ teaspoon light brown sugar
¼ teaspoon salt
1 sheet frozen vegan puff pastry, thawed

Preheat the oven to 400°F. In a small bowl, combine the cashews, curry powder, coriander, cumin, brown sugar, and salt. Mix well and set aside.

Roll out the pastry on a work surface and brush the top lightly with water. Coat evenly with the reserved seasoning mixture. Place a sheet of parchment paper, waxed paper, or plastic wrap over the pastry and use a rolling pin to press the nuts and spices into the pastry so they adhere.

With a sharp knife or a pizza cutter, cut the pastry into two pieces, about 5 by 10 inches each. Cut each piece into ½ by 5-inch strips. Pick up each strip and twist to create a spiral "straw" and arrange on a baking sheet. Repeat with the remaining pastry strips. Bake until the pastry is golden brown, about 15 minutes. Serve warm.

note: If unsalted cashews are unavailable, use salted cashews, but omit or reduce the amount of salt used.

provençal stuffed mushrooms

makes 16

Experience the exciting flavors of Provence all stuffed inside succulent mushrooms. A great appetizer when made with smaller mushrooms, you can also stuff the filling inside four large portobellos for a delectable main dish serving 4.

1 tablespoon olive oil
3 cloves garlic, minced
2 scallions, minced
16 cremini mushroom caps, stems removed and chopped
1 large roasted red bell pepper (see page 16), or 1 (6-ounce) jar, drained and minced

2 tablespoons minced oil-packed sun-dried tomatoes
1 teaspoon herbes de Provence
Salt and freshly ground black pepper
3 to 4 tablespoons dried bread crumbs

Preheat the oven to 400°F. Heat the oil in a skillet over medium heat. Add the garlic and scallions and cook until softened, 30 seconds. Add the mushroom stems, bell pepper, sun-dried tomatoes, herbes de Provence, and salt and pepper to taste. Cook, stirring, until the mixture is softened, and well combined, about 3 minutes. Remove from the heat and sprinkle on the bread crumbs, stirring to mix. Taste and adjust the seasonings.

Stuff the mushroom caps with the stuffing and arrange in a greased shallow baking pan. Bake until the mushrooms are tender and the stuffing is hot, about 18 minutes. Serve hot.

vegetable fritters

serves 4 to 6

These easy and versatile fritters can be made with any combination of vegetables you desire. It's a great way to use up leftover cooked veggies—just chop them up and add to the batter. You can also swap out about ¼ cup of the all-purpose flour for chickpea flour or cornmeal, for a slightly different flavor. I like to serve the fritters with vegan sour cream spiked with a little Tabasco or other hot sauce. In addition to being a good appetizer, they make a great side dish.

¾ cup all-purpose flour
½ teaspoon baking powder
½ teaspoon salt
¼ teaspoon freshly ground black pepper
½ cup nondairy milk
1 yellow onion, shredded

1 small Yukon Gold potato, shredded
1 cup frozen corn kernels, thawed
½ cup frozen peas, thawed
2 tablespoons minced fresh parsley
1 tablespoon olive oil

Preheat the oven to 250°F. In a bowl, combine the flour, baking powder, salt, and pepper. Stir in the nondairy milk, onion, potato, corn, peas, and parsley and mix well to combine. The mixture should be thick.

Heat the oil in a large nonstick skillet over medium heat. Spoon 2 tablespoons of the mixture onto the hot skillet and flatten with the back of your spoon. Repeat to make as many fritters as will fit comfortably in your pan without crowding. Cook, flipping once, until browned on both sides, about 8 minutes total. Transfer the cooked fritters to a heatproof plate and keep hot in the oven while you cook the remaining fritters. Serve hot.

easy artichoke puffs

serves 4 to 6

This delicious and elegant appetizer can be assembled quickly with on-hand ingredients. For an even faster version, instead of puff pastry, spoon the filling into small bite-size phyllo cups available in the freezer case of most supermarkets.

1 sheet frozen vegan puff pastry, thawed
1 teaspoon olive oil
¼ cup minced scallions
1 (6-ounce) jar marinated artichoke hearts, drained and finely chopped
2 tablespoons finely minced oil-packed sun-dried tomatoes

1 teaspoon capers
3 tablespoons vegan cream cheese
⅛ teaspoon red pepper flakes (optional)
Salt and freshly ground black pepper

Preheat the oven to 400°F. Line a baking sheet with parchment paper or a silicone baking mat and set aside. Unfold the pastry onto a flat surface. Use a knife to cut the pastry into 16 or so squares or use a 2 to 3-inch cookie cutter to cut it into circles or other shapes. Arrange the pieces of pastry on the prepared baking sheet. Bake until puffed and golden brown, about 10 minutes. Remove from the oven and set aside. Reduce the oven temperature to 375°F.

While the pastry is baking, heat the oil in a skillet over medium heat. Add the scallions and cook until softened, about 3 minutes. Add the artichokes, tomatoes, capers, cream cheese, and red pepper flakes, if using. Season to taste with salt and pepper and stir to mix well. Remove the pan from the heat.

Use your finger to press an indentation into the center of each baked pastry puff. Spoon the artichoke mixture into the centers of the pastry puffs. Bake until hot, 5 minutes. Serve hot.

jerk-spiced kale crisps

serves 4 to 6

Recipes for kale chips seem to be popping up all over. It's great to see people so excited about eating their veggies. Although crispy kale is often served plain or with just a touch of salt, I prefer to spice mine up by sprinkling them with a jerk spice blend. If your jerk seasoning blend doesn't contain salt, you might want to add a little extra. Watch the kale carefully when baking so it doesn't burn—the time it takes to bake will depend on the type of kale used.

1 bunch kale
1 tablespoon olive oil
1 teaspoon jerk spice blend
Salt

Preheat the oven to 350°F. Remove the tough stems from the kale and discard. Be sure your kale is dry after you wash it (use a salad spinner to do this). Tear the kale leaves into bite-size pieces and arrange on 1 or 2 baking sheets in a single layer. Bake until crisp, 10 to 15 minutes, depending on the type of kale used. Curly kale takes 15 minutes; more fragile kale takes about 10 minutes. Be careful not to burn.

Transfer the kale to a large bowl and drizzle with the olive oil. Sprinkle with the jerk spice blend and season with salt to taste. Toss gently to coat. Serve immediately. Do not refrigerate.

super nachos

I call these nachos "super" not just because they're super-good but because they include a bottom layer of zesty pinto beans and salsa, making them satisfying enough to enjoy as a meal. Of course, they make a "super" snack, too!

1½ cups home-cooked pinto beans,
   or 1 (15-ounce) can, drained and rinsed
1 cup tomato salsa
1½ teaspoons chili powder
Salt and freshly ground black pepper
1 ripe Hass avocado
⅓ cup nutritional yeast
2 tablespoons all-purpose flour
1 tablespoon mellow white miso paste
1 tablespoon freshly squeezed lemon juice
1 teaspoon prepared mustard
½ teaspoon onion powder
¼ teaspoon ground cumin
¾ cup nondairy milk
6 cups tortilla chips

GARNISHES
½ cup vegan sour cream
⅓ cup sliced black olives
¼ cup pickled jalapeño slices
2 tablespoons minced scallions

Preheat the oven to 400°F. Grease a 9-inch baking dish and set aside. In a small saucepan, combine the pinto beans, ½ cup of the salsa, and 1 teaspoon of the chili powder, and salt and pepper to taste. Cook, stirring, until well mixed, mashing the beans somewhat to break up and become creamy, about 4 minutes. Spread the bean mixture in the bottom of the prepared baking dish and set aside. Halve and pit the avocado, spoon out the flesh, and chop. Set aside.

In a small skillet, combine the nutritional yeast, flour, miso, lemon juice, mustard, onion powder, cumin, the remaining ½ teaspoon chili powder, and the nondairy milk. Season to taste with salt and pepper. Cook, stirring, over medium heat until the sauce thickens, about 4 minutes.

Spread the tortilla chips on top of the bean mixture, then spoon the sauce over the tortilla chips and bake the nachos until hot, 5 minutes. Spoon the remaining ½ cup salsa on the nachos and top with the reserved avocado. Garnish with the sour cream, olives, jalapeños, and scallions. Serve immediately.

stovetop

suppers

If you're looking for a great no-fuss meal that you can get on the table in 30 minutes, you've come to the right place. With satisfying grain dishes such as Quinoa and Chard with Sherry-Glazed Mushrooms, and Chipotle Corn and Quinoa with Pintos, plus hearty bean and vegetable dishes including Moroccan Chickpeas and Spinach, and Shortcut Mushroom–Artichoke Risotto, you'll find that "quick and easy" can also mean "flavorful and nutritious."

Featuring recipes from around the globe such as Coconut-Curry Chickpeas and Cauliflower, Korean Hot Pot, and Lebanese Sleek, your taste buds will never get tired.

Ideal for busy weeknights, several of these recipes are one-dish meals in themselves, while others need little more than a quick-cooking grain or pasta, or roasted or steamed vegetable, as accompaniments. Many of these recipes, including Ginger-Sesame Seitan with Spicy Basil Snow Peas and Tempeh with Mellow Mustard Sauce, also make great company fare.

lemony couscous
and white bean pilaf

serves 4

Quick-cooking couscous combines with beans and shredded vegetables for an easy one-dish meal made even better with fragrant basil and lemon juice.

1 tablespoon olive oil
1 large carrot, grated
1 zucchini, grated
3 cloves garlic, minced
3 scallions, minced
1¼ cups couscous
2½ cups vegetable broth
Grated zest and juice of 1 lemon

1½ cups home-cooked cannellini or other white beans, or 1 (15-ounce) can, drained and rinsed
½ cup oil-packed sun-dried tomatoes, cut into strips
2 tablespoons minced fresh basil or parsley
Salt and freshly ground black pepper

Heat the oil in a saucepan over medium heat. Add the carrot, zucchini, garlic, and scallions and cook until softened, 2 minutes. Stir in the couscous, broth, and lemon zest, and bring to a boil. Remove from the heat, cover, and set aside for 10 minutes. Add the lemon juice, beans, sun-dried tomatoes, basil, and salt and pepper to taste. Stir gently to combine. Serve hot.

lebanese sleek

serves 4

I developed this satisfying recipe for a friend who enjoyed it in a Lebanese restaurant and wanted to make it at home. The name of this pilaf comes from the word *silek*, which is Arabic for Swiss chard. It reminds me of a Middle Eastern version of hoppin' John. Serve this topped with Tzatziki Sauce (page 118).

½ cup medium-grind bulgur
1¼ cups hot vegetable broth
1 tablespoon olive oil
1 large yellow onion, finely chopped
1½ to 2 teaspoons zataar or baharat spice blend (see note)

9 ounces chard or kale, chopped
4 scallions, chopped
1½ cups home-cooked black-eyed peas, or 1 (15-ounce) can, drained and rinsed
2 tablespoons freshly squeezed lemon juice
Salt and freshly ground black pepper

Place the bulgur in a bowl. Add the vegetable broth and set aside for 15 minutes.

Heat the oil in a large skillet over medium heat. Add the onion and spice blend to taste and cook until the onion is softened, about 5 minutes. Add the chard, scallions, black-eyed peas, and the soaked bulgur. Reduce the heat to low, cover, and simmer until the ingredients are tender and the flavors are well blended, about 10 minutes. Stir in the lemon juice and season to taste with salt and pepper. Taste and adjust the spice blend, if needed. Serve hot.

note: Zataar or baharat spice blends are available in Middle Eastern markets, gourmet grocers, or spice stores. They are also available online. If unavailable, combine the following: ½ teaspoon each paprika and freshly ground black pepper, ¼ teaspoon each ground coriander and ground cumin, ⅛ teaspoon each ground nutmeg, cloves, and cinnamon.

shortcut mushroom–artichoke risotto

serves 4

I love a good risotto, but it's notoriously time-consuming to make. That's why I came up with this shortcut version that starts with cooked brown rice and incorporates a flavorful broth thickened with white beans. Even though the method is unorthodox, the results are creamy and delicious. Testers couldn't believe how much this tastes like risotto made "the hard way." If you happen to have white truffle oil on hand, drizzle a little on top before serving.

1 tablespoon olive oil
1 small yellow onion, chopped
1 clove garlic, crushed
¾ cup home-cooked or canned white beans
1 cup vegetable broth
8 ounces cremini mushrooms, thinly sliced
3 scallions, minced

3 cups cooked brown rice
1 (6-ounce) jar marinated artichoke hearts, drained and chopped
2 tablespoons dry white wine or freshly squeezed lemon juice
Salt and freshly ground black pepper
2 tablespoons minced fresh parsley

Heat ½ tablespoon of the oil in a skillet over medium heat. Add the onion and garlic, cover, and cook for 5 minutes, or until softened. Transfer to a blender or food processor, add the beans and vegetable broth, and blend until smooth. Set aside.

Heat the remaining ½ tablespoon oil in the same skillet over medium heat. Add the mushrooms and cook until softened, about 3 minutes. Add the scallions, cooked rice, and artichokes. Stir in the bean mixture and cook, stirring, until hot and well blended, about 10 minutes. Stir in the wine and season to taste with salt and pepper. Serve hot sprinkled with the parsley.

zucchini frittata

serves 4

My mother often served a zucchini frittata (made with eggs) for a light Sunday supper, accompanied by toasted Italian bread. I sometimes continue the tradition with this vegan version (made with tofu) that can be on the table in less than 30 minutes. It also makes a terrific brunch dish.

1 tablespoon olive oil
1 small yellow onion, minced
2 cups shredded zucchini (1 medium zucchini)
2 cloves garlic, minced
Salt and freshly ground black pepper
1 pound firm tofu, well drained
¼ cup nondairy milk

3 tablespoons nutritional yeast
1 tablespoon cornstarch
1 teaspoon onion powder
1 teaspoon dried basil
¼ teaspoon ground turmeric
1 small ripe tomato, chopped
⅓ cup pitted kalamata olives, chopped
2 tablespoons chopped fresh basil

Heat the oil in an ovenproof skillet. Add the onion, cover, and cook until tender, about 5 minutes. Add the zucchini and garlic and cook, stirring occasionally, until softened, about 3 minutes. Season to taste with salt and pepper. Set aside.

In a blender, combine the tofu, nondairy milk, nutritional yeast, cornstarch, onion powder, dried basil, and turmeric. Add ½ teaspoon salt and pepper to taste and blend until smooth.

Preheat the broiler. Spread the tofu mixture evenly over the vegetables in the ovenproof skillet. Cover and cook over medium heat until firm and golden brown on the bottom, about 15 minutes. Run under the broiler just long enough for the top to become golden brown. Cut into wedges and sprinkle the top with the tomato, olives, and fresh basil. Serve hot.

green chile–tofu migas

serves 4

Tofu stands in for eggs in this vegan version of the popular Tex-Mex skillet dish. Made with pieces of corn tortilla, it's a great way to use leftover tortillas. Optional toppings include vegan sour cream, tomato salsa, avocado, and hot sauce. Serve with a pile of home-fried potatoes for a satisfying meal anytime. This flavorful dish can be made hot or mild, depending on your own heat tolerance; just use your choice of hot or mild salsa and hot or mild green chiles. You can substitute a fresh jalapeño in place of the canned chopped green chiles, if you prefer.

1 pound soft tofu, drained
2 tablespoons nutritional yeast
½ teaspoon salt
⅓ cup tomato salsa
1 ripe avocado
1 tablespoon olive oil
1 small yellow onion, minced
2 cloves garlic, minced
2 scallions, minced
4 (6-inch) corn tortillas, torn into bite-size pieces

1 (4-ounce) can chopped green chiles, hot or mild, drained
1 tomato, chopped
1 tablespoon minced fresh cilantro

OPTIONAL TOPPINGS
½ cup vegan sour cream
Additional tomato salsa
Avocado
Hot sauce

Place the tofu in a bowl and mash well. Add the nutritional yeast, salt, and salsa and mix until well combined. Halve and pit the avocado, spoon out the flesh, and chop. Set aside.

Heat the oil in a large skillet over medium heat. Add the onion and cook until softened, 5 minutes. Add the garlic, scallions, and tortilla pieces and cook until fragrant, 2 minutes. Stir in the chiles and the reserved tofu mixture and cook, stirring, until hot and well combined, 5 minutes. Add the chopped tomato and cilantro and stir to combine. Taste and adjust the seasonings.

Serve hot topped with sour cream, additional salsa, the reserved avocado, and the hot sauce.

tofu "scampi" with spinach

serves 4

Before we went vegan, shrimp "scampi" was a favorite dish at our house. I now enjoy the same preparation with crisp chunks of golden tofu, which takes on the flavors of the garlic, lemon, and other seasonings. The optional dulse flakes add extra nutrients and a taste of the sea, but it's wonderful without it, too. Spinach provides a lovely color contrast and saves you the time of preparing a separate vegetable. When served over rice, quinoa, or pasta, you can have a delicious meal in minutes.

1½ tablespoons olive oil
4 cloves garlic, minced
1 (9-ounce) bag fresh baby spinach
2 teaspoons dulse flakes (optional, see headnote)
1 teaspoon dried basil
½ teaspoon dried oregano
Salt and freshly ground black pepper
3 tablespoons cornstarch
1 pound extra-firm tofu, drained and cut into 1-inch dice
2 tablespoons freshly squeezed lemon juice
2 tablespoons dry white wine

Heat ½ tablespoon of oil in a large skillet over medium heat. Add the garlic, spinach, dulse, if using, basil, and oregano, and season to taste with salt and pepper. Cook, stirring, until the spinach is wilted, about 3 minutes. Remove from the skillet and set aside.

In a shallow bowl, combine the cornstarch, ½ teaspoon salt, and ¼ teaspoon pepper. Mix well. Add the tofu and toss gently to coat. Heat the remaining 1 tablespoon oil in the same skillet over medium-high heat. Add the tofu and cook until golden brown. Return the spinach mixture to the skillet and toss to combine with the tofu. Add the lemon juice and wine. Taste and adjust the seasonings. Serve hot.

tropical quinoa and black beans

serves 4

This dramatically colorful dish is flavored with a variety of seasonings for a taste of the tropics. A splash of fresh lime juice when ready to serve brightens the flavors even more. If you prefer extra heat, add a minced hot jalapeño or serrano chile in addition to or instead of the cayenne. Cooked brown rice may be used instead of the cooked quinoa.

1 cup quinoa, well rinsed
1 ripe mango
1 tablespoon neutral vegetable oil
1 small red onion, minced
½ red bell pepper, minced
2 teaspoons grated fresh ginger
2 cloves garlic, minced
1 teaspoon light brown sugar
½ teaspoon dried thyme
¼ teaspoon ground cumin

¼ teaspoon ground allspice
¼ teaspoon ground coriander
⅛ teaspoon cayenne
1½ cups home-cooked black beans, or 1 (15-ounce) can, drained and rinsed
Salt and freshly ground black pepper
2 tablespoons minced fresh cilantro
1 to 2 tablespoons freshly squeezed lime juice
Lime wedges, for serving (optional)

Cook the quinoa in a saucepan of boiling salted water until tender, 15 to 20 minutes. Drain and set aside. Slice through the mango lengthwise, next to one side of the flat pit, and detach; repeat for the other side. Spoon out the flesh and chop. Set aside.

While the quinoa is cooking, heat the oil in a large skillet over medium heat. Add the onion and bell pepper and cook until softened, about 4 minutes. Stir in the ginger, garlic, sugar, thyme, cumin, allspice, coriander, and cayenne and cook, stirring, until fragrant, 1 minute. Add the beans and reserved quinoa, and season to taste with salt and pepper. Stir in the reserved mango, cilantro, and lime juice, and cook until heated through, 2 to 3 minutes. Serve hot with the lime wedges, if using.

coconut-curry chickpeas and cauliflower

serves 4

Coconut milk adds richness to the flavorful sauce that can be made hot or mild, depending on the curry powder or paste that you use. Serve over freshly cooked basmati rice.

1 tablespoon neutral vegetable oil
1 small yellow onion, minced
1 carrot, thinly sliced
3 cups small cauliflower florets (from
   1 small cauliflower)
2 tablespoons curry powder or paste, or
   more
1 (14.5-ounce) can diced tomatoes, drained

1 cup vegetable broth
1½ cups home-cooked chickpeas, or
   1 (15-ounce) can, drained and rinsed
1 cup frozen peas
1 (13-ounce) can unsweetened
   coconut milk
½ teaspoon salt
Freshly ground black pepper

Heat the oil in a large saucepan over medium heat. Add the onion, cover, and cook until softened, about 5 minutes. Stir in the carrot, cauliflower, and curry powder to taste. Add the tomatoes and broth, cover, and cook until the vegetables are softened, about 10 minutes. Stir in the chickpeas, peas, coconut milk, salt, and pepper to taste. Cook uncovered until the flavors are well blended and the mixture thickens slightly, about 10 minutes longer. Serve hot.

white beans with mushrooms and sauerkraut

serves 4

This stick-to-your-ribs recipe was inspired by two delicious eastern European soups, one made with white beans and the other with mushrooms and sauerkraut. Those ingredients combine in this skillet dish along with a splash of white wine, dill, and vegan sour cream. Served over noodles, it's a quick and hearty meal for a cold winter night.

1 tablespoon neutral vegetable oil
1 large yellow onion, chopped
1 carrot, thinly sliced
8 ounces white mushrooms, sliced
2 tablespoons sweet Hungarian paprika
2 tablespoons all-purpose flour
1 tablespoon tomato paste
1 cup vegetable broth
¼ cup dry white wine

1 (15-ounce) can sauerkraut, drained and rinsed
3 cups home-cooked white beans, or 2 (15-ounce) cans, drained and rinsed
1 tablespoon minced fresh dill, or 2 teaspoons dried
Salt and freshly ground black pepper
½ cup vegan sour cream
Freshly cooked egg-free noodles

Heat the oil in a large skillet over medium heat. Add the onion and carrot. Cover and cook until the vegetables are tender, about 7 minutes. Add the mushrooms and cook until softened, 2 minutes, then stir in the paprika and flour, and cook, stirring, 2 minutes longer to remove the raw taste from the flour. Stir in the tomato paste, then stir in the vegetable broth, wine, sauerkraut, beans, and dill. Season to taste with salt and pepper and bring to a boil. Reduce the heat to medium and simmer, stirring occasionally, until hot and the vegetables are soft, about 10 minutes. When ready to serve, remove from the heat and stir in the sour cream. Serve immediately over noodles.

jerk seitan and vegetable skillet

serves 4

The bold flavors of Jamaican jerk spices envelop chunks of seitan and vegetables in this vibrant dish. I like to serve this over freshly cooked quinoa, but it's also great with rice or couscous. This is a really versatile recipe—you can swap out tofu or tempeh for the seitan and use different vegetables, if you like (cauliflower or broccoli are good here). As a side note, unlike the dark brown jerk sauces you usually see, this sauce is decidedly green in color (owing to the scallions and jalapeño).

JERK SAUCE
6 scallions, coarsely chopped
1 jalapeño or other hot chile, halved and
  seeded
1 large clove garlic, crushed
1 teaspoon chopped fresh ginger
3 tablespoons soy sauce
1 tablespoon cider vinegar
Juice of 1 lime
1 tablespoon dark brown sugar
1 teaspoon fresh thyme leaves, or
  ½ teaspoon dried
1 teaspoon ground allspice

½ teaspoon salt
¼ teaspoon freshly ground black pepper
¼ teaspoon ground cumin
¼ teaspoon ground nutmeg
¼ cup freshly squeezed orange juice

SEITAN AND VEGETABLES
2 tablespoons olive oil
8 ounces seitan, cut into bite-size pieces
1 red onion, chopped
1 red or yellow bell pepper, chopped
1 zucchini, chopped
1 cup grape tomatoes, halved

For the jerk sauce, in a blender, combine all the ingredients for the sauce and blend until smooth. Set aside.

For the seitan and vegetables, heat 1 tablespoon of the oil in a large skillet over medium heat. Add the seitan and cook until browned, about 7 minutes. Remove from the skillet and set aside. Reheat the skillet with the remaining 1 tablespoon oil. Add the onion, bell pepper, and zucchini and cook until softened, stirring occasionally, about 5 minutes. Return the seitan to the skillet. Pour on the jerk sauce and cook, stirring gently until the seitan is coated with the sauce. Add a few tablespoons of water if the mixture is too dry. Add the tomatoes and cook until just softened, about 5 minutes. Serve hot.

ginger–sesame seitan with spicy basil snow peas

serves 4

This flavorful stir-fry is as versatile as it is delicious. Here are just a few ways to change it up: use extra-firm tofu or tempeh instead of seitan; add thin slices of red bell pepper; substitute lightly steamed broccoli or green beans for the snow peas; use mint or cilantro leaves in place of the Thai basil. This is delicious served over freshly cooked rice or tossed with hot cooked spaghetti or rice noodles. Add more soy sauce and sriracha to taste.

1½ tablespoons neutral vegetable oil
12 ounces seitan, cut into ½ by 2-inch strips
5 scallions, chopped
2 cloves garlic, minced
2 teaspoons grated fresh ginger
8 ounces snow peas

2 tablespoons soy sauce
2 teaspoons sriracha sauce or other Asian
  chili sauce
1 teaspoon toasted sesame oil
¼ cup Thai basil leaves
2 tablespoons toasted sesame seeds

Heat ½ tablespoon of the vegetable oil in a large skillet over medium-high heat. Add the seitan and stir-fry until browned, about 5 minutes. Remove the seitan from the skillet and set aside.

Return the skillet to the heat and add the remaining 1 tablespoon vegetable oil. Add the scallions, garlic, ginger, and snow peas and stir-fry until the snow peas are crisp-tender, about 3 minutes. Add the soy sauce, sriracha, sesame oil, basil, and sesame seeds and stir-fry until fragrant, 1 minute. Return the seitan to the skillet and stir-fry with the other ingredients until hot. Serve immediately.

tofu skillet scramble

serves 4

I think what sends this tofu scramble to the head of its class are the ground fennel seed and crushed red pepper flakes that give the scramble a faintly sausagelike flavor. Of course, it may also be the inclusion of a chopped baked potato which is like having your scramble and home fries all in one. The roasted bell pepper, scallions, and sun-dried tomatoes make a good thing even better.

1 pound firm tofu, drained
¼ cup nutritional yeast
1 tablespoon soy sauce
½ teaspoon garlic powder
½ teaspoon smoked paprika
¼ teaspoon ground turmeric
Salt and freshly ground black pepper
1 tablespoon olive oil

5 scallions, minced
1 leftover baked russet potato, chopped (see note)
1 roasted red bell pepper (see page 16), chopped
3 oil-packed sun-dried tomatoes, minced
½ teaspoon ground fennel seed
½ teaspoon red pepper flakes

In a bowl, combine the tofu, nutritional yeast, soy sauce, garlic powder, paprika, turmeric, ½ teaspoon salt, and ¼ teaspoon pepper. Mash the tofu and mix together until well combined. Set aside.

Heat the oil in a large skillet over medium heat. Add the scallions and potato and cook until the scallions are softened and the potatoes are lightly browned, about 5 minutes. Add the bell pepper, sun-dried tomatoes, fennel, red pepper flakes, and salt and pepper to taste. Add the tofu mixture and mix well to combine. Cook, turning portions of the mixture with a metal spatula until the flavors are well combined and the mixture is hot, about 10 minutes. Serve hot.

note: If you don't have a leftover baked potato, you can "bake" one in the microwave until just tender, about 5 minutes.

indonesian vegetable and tofu scramble

serves 4

The flavors of Southeast Asia figure prominently in this unusual but delicious scramble. I like to serve it with wedges of sesame-scallion pancakes (available in the freezer section at Asian markets) for a quick and satisfying meal.

2 tablespoons hoisin sauce
2 tablespoons soy sauce
1 tablespoon water
2 teaspoons ground coriander
1 teaspoon curry powder
½ teaspoon ground cumin
Cayenne
1 pound extra-firm tofu, drained and diced or crumbled

1 tablespoon neutral vegetable oil
1 small yellow onion, chopped
1 carrot, thinly sliced
2 to 3 cloves garlic, minced
2 teaspoons grated fresh ginger
4 cups finely chopped bok choy
½ cup frozen peas
Salt and freshly ground black pepper

In a medium bowl, combine the hoisin sauce, soy sauce, water, coriander, curry powder, and cumin. Add cayenne to taste. Stir until well mixed. Add the tofu and toss gently to coat. Set aside.

Heat the oil in a large skillet over medium heat. Add the onion and carrot. Cover and cook until softened, 5 minutes. Remove the lid and stir in the garlic, ginger, and bok choy. Cook, stirring, until the bok choy is wilted, about 4 minutes. Add the reserved tofu mixture and the peas. Season to taste with salt and pepper. Cook, stirring gently to combine and heat through, about 7 minutes. If the mixture is too dry, add a splash of water. Taste and adjust the seasonings. Serve hot.

spicy smoked portobello tacos

serves 4

Finely chopped portobello mushrooms have the perfect texture for taco filling. Their ability to absorb the smoky hot flavors of the chipotle-infused sauce ensures a wonderful flavor as well. Assemble the tacos any way you like, with lettuce, salsa, chopped tomato, and the cooling contrast of avocado or vegan sour cream.

2 chipotle chiles in adobo, finely minced
2 tablespoons soy sauce
1½ tablespoons agave nectar or maple syrup
½ teaspoon Liquid Smoke
¼ teaspoon smoked paprika
1 ripe avocado
1 tablespoon olive oil

4 to 5 large portobello mushrooms, finely chopped
8 (7-inch) flour tortillas
2 cups shredded lettuce
1 cup tomato salsa
1 large ripe tomato, chopped
½ cup vegan sour cream

In a small bowl, combine the chiles, soy sauce, agave, ½ teaspoon Liquid Smoke or to taste, and the paprika. Set aside. Halve and pit the avocado, spoon out the flesh, and chop. Set aside.

Heat the oil in a skillet over medium heat. Add the mushrooms and cook, stirring, until the mushrooms soften and most of the liquid they release is evaporated, 5 to 7 minutes. Add the reserved sauce, stirring to mix well. Cook to heat through and blend the flavors, a few minutes longer. Keep warm. Warm the tortillas and keep warm.

Set out bowls containing the lettuce, salsa, tomato, the reserved avocado, and the sour cream. Transfer the mushroom mixture to a bowl and serve with the warm tortillas and the accompaniments.

chipotle corn and quinoa with pintos

serves 4

Quinoa is the ultimate quick-fix grain. It cooks up in 15 minutes, is a protein-rich nutritional powerhouse, and has a great nutty taste. What's not to love? In this recipe, quinoa teams up with corn, pintos, and chipotles for a delightful Southwest flavor. For less heat, use only one chipotle instead of two.

1 tablespoon olive oil
1 yellow onion, chopped
3 cloves garlic, minced
1 cup quinoa, rinsed and drained
1½ cups fresh or frozen corn kernels
1½ cups home-cooked pinto beans, or
    1 (15-ounce) can, drained and rinsed

2 chipotle chiles in adobo, minced
2 cups vegetable broth
Salt
¼ teaspoon freshly ground black pepper
½ cup chopped fresh cilantro
2 scallions, minced

Heat the oil in a saucepan over medium heat. Add the onion, cover, and cook until softened, 5 minutes. Stir in the garlic, then add the quinoa and cook, stirring, until lightly toasted, 1 to 2 minutes. Add the corn, beans, chiles, and broth. Season with salt to taste and the pepper. Bring to a boil, then reduce the heat to a simmer, cover, and cook until the quinoa is tender, about 15 minutes. Stir in the cilantro and scallions. Taste and adjust the seasonings. Serve hot.

seitan donburi with unagi sauce

serves 4

My prevegan days often found me in Japanese restaurants where, among other things, I sometimes ordered unagi sushi and donburi. I have combined what I liked most about those two dishes: seitan coated in a hauntingly flavorful "unagi" sauce served over hot cooked rice, donburi style. Serve with a cooked leafy green such as stir-fried baby bok choy for a complete meal. Keep some cooked rice on hand to heat up when ready to serve.

¼ cup soy sauce
¼ cup sake or mirin (sweet rice wine)
2 tablespoons agave nectar or sugar
1 tablespoon neutral vegetable oil

12 ounces seitan, cut into ¼-inch strips
3 to 4 scallions, minced
3 cups hot cooked rice
Toasted sesame seeds, for garnish

In a small bowl, combine the soy sauce, sake, and agave, stirring to blend. Set aside.

Heat the oil in a large skillet over medium-high heat. Add the seitan and cook, stirring, until browned, about 7 minutes. Add the scallions and cook until softened, 1 minute longer. Add the reserved sauce and continue to cook, stirring, until the seitan is well coated, 5 minutes.

To serve, spoon the rice into individual bowls, top with the seitan and sauce, and garnish with the sesame seeds.

moroccan chickpeas
with tomatoes and spinach

serves 4 to 6

A Moroccan spice blend adds a distinctive flavor to this quick sauté. Served over couscous, it can be on the table in just minutes. If you don't have a ready-made spice blend, instructions for making your own follow this recipe (see note). If you don't have a pot large enough to contain the volume of spinach, simply microwave the spinach for a minute or two in a covered bowl to reduce the volume.

1 tablespoon olive oil
1 yellow onion, chopped
1 small red bell pepper, chopped
4 cloves garlic, minced
4 teaspoons Moroccan spice blend
   (see note)

9 ounces baby spinach
2 (14.5-ounce) cans diced tomatoes,
   including juice
3 cups home-cooked chickpeas, or
   2 (15-ounce) cans, drained and rinsed
Salt and freshly ground black pepper

Heat the oil in a large pot over medium heat. Add the onion, bell pepper, and garlic. Cover and cook until softened, 5 minutes. Stir in the spice blend, then add the spinach, the tomatoes and their juice, and the chickpeas. Season to taste with salt and pepper. Cook, stirring, until the vegetables are tender and the flavors are well blended, 12 to 15 minutes. Taste and adjust the seasonings. Serve hot.

note: Moroccan spice blends can contain up to 50 different spices. Look for them at gourmet grocers or online. If unavailable, combine the following spices to use instead:

1 teaspoon ground coriander
1 teaspoon ground ginger
½ teaspoon ground allspice
½ teaspoon ground cinnamon
½ teaspoon ground cumin
¼ teaspoon ground turmeric
⅛ teaspoon cayenne
⅛ teaspoon ground nutmeg

korean hot pot

serves 4

This meal is fun to eat because everyone cooks their own food right at the table, making it more of a "tabletop" dinner rather than "stovetop," although the broth does get heated on the stovetop prior to serving. In this recipe, the vegetables and broth are served over hot cooked rice. It's also great served with Asian Vegetable Pancakes (see page 58).

6 cups vegetable broth
1 head bok choy, thinly sliced
1 pound extra-firm tofu, diced
12 to 16 small shiitake mushroom caps
2 cups bean sprouts
1½ cups snow peas
1 tablespoon kochujang paste (Korean chili paste) (optional)
3 cups hot cooked rice

TOPPINGS
Toasted sesame seeds
Minced scallions
Soy sauce
Peanut sauce

Bring the broth to a simmer in a Dutch oven or heatproof earthenware pot over medium heat (see note). Once it is hot, place the pot of broth in the center of the table over a heat source (a single-burner butane stove works well for this). Arrange the bok choy, tofu, mushrooms, bean sprouts, and snow peas on a platter and set on the table near the simmering hot pot. Transfer some of each of the ingredients into the broth to cook. For a spicy broth, you can add a spoonful of kochujang paste. Set out the toppings on the table in small bowls.

Spoon some rice into the bottom of individual soup bowls. Instruct diners to select ingredients from the hot pot to add to the rice and to garnish their serving with toppings of choice. As the cooked ingredients are removed and eaten, add more of the raw ingredients to the hot pot.

note: A variety of heatproof earthenware pots can be found in Asian markets and online. These pots can be used directly over a gas flame and are ideal for cooking on a tabletop butane stove. If you don't have a ceramic pot, you can use a regular Dutch oven instead. Another option for tabletop cooking is an electric multicooker, which is similar to a slow cooker but can cook at higher temperatures and is wider and more shallow.

asian vegetable pancakes

serves 4

This recipe makes four medium pancakes, but you could make two large or eight small ones, instead. Hint: The small to medium ones are easier to flip, but if you make larger ones, you can cut them right in the pan for easier flipping.

DIPPING SAUCE
¼ cup soy sauce
3 tablespoons rice vinegar
2 tablespoons mirin or sake
2 tablespoons water
1 teaspoon toasted sesame oil
1 teaspoon hot chili oil, or ½ teaspoon red pepper flakes
1 teaspoon grated fresh ginger
1 teaspoon sugar

PANCAKES
½ cup all-purpose flour
2 tablespoons rice flour
2 tablespoons tapioca flour or potato starch
¾ teaspoon salt
1 teaspoon sesame seeds
1 cup water
1½ cups minced scallions (about 6 scallions)
1½ cups finely chopped bok choy or napa cabbage
½ teaspoon red pepper flakes
Neutral vegetable oil, for frying

To make the dipping sauce, in a small bowl, combine all the sauce ingredients and mix well. Set aside. You should have about ¾ cup.

To make the pancakes, in a medium bowl, combine the all-purpose flour, rice flour, tapioca flour, salt, and sesame seeds. Stir in the water and mix until blended. Add the scallions, bok choy, and red pepper flakes, and stir to combine.

Preheat the oven to 250°F. Heat a thin layer of oil in a large nonstick skillet over medium-high heat. Ladle one-quarter of the batter into the hot skillet, tilting the pan to spread it thinly. Reduce the heat to medium and cook until firm and nicely browned on the bottom, 5 to 7 minutes. Flip the pancakes to cook the other side until browned, about 3 minutes longer. Transfer the cooked pancake to a baking sheet and keep warm in the oven while you cook the remaining pancakes, adding more oil to the pan, if needed. Serve hot with the dipping sauce on the side. For convenience, divide the sauce into small individual bowls for each person at the table.

smoky chipotle–chocolate chili

serves 4

The addition of unsweetened chocolate gives this chili a rich depth and balances the acidity of the tomatoes. Chipotle chiles in adobo add their special smoky heat. A green salad and cornbread are ideal accompaniments.

1 tablespoon olive oil
1 yellow onion, finely chopped
4 cloves garlic, minced
2 tablespoons grated unsweetened
    chocolate
2 tablespoons chili powder
1 teaspoon ground cumin
1 teaspoon smoked paprika
½ teaspoon dried oregano
1 teaspoon dark brown sugar

1 teaspoon salt
¼ teaspoon freshly ground black pepper
1 (14.5-ounce) can diced tomatoes,
    including juice
1 (14.5-ounce) can crushed tomatoes
2 canned chipotle chiles in adobo, minced
3 cups home-cooked black beans, or
    2 (15-ounce) cans, drained and rinsed
1 cup vegetable broth or water

Heat the oil in a large pot over medium heat. Add the onion and garlic. Cover and cook until softened, about 5 minutes. Stir in the chocolate, chili powder, cumin, paprika, oregano, sugar, salt, and pepper. Add the diced tomatoes, crushed tomatoes, and chiles and stir until well blended. Add the beans and broth and bring to a boil. Reduce the heat to medium-low and simmer uncovered, stirring occasionally, until the chili thickens and the flavors have developed, 20 to 25 minutes. Taste and adjust the seasonings. Serve hot.

quinoa and chard with sherry-glazed mushrooms

serves 4

Succulent sherry-glazed mushrooms transform an unassuming grain and greens dish into a spectacular meal. Quinoa is especially protein rich, but if you prefer more substance in this recipe, a cup of cooked white beans or slivers of seitan can be added to the mushrooms.

1 cup quinoa, well rinsed
2 cups vegetable broth
Salt
6 ounces chard, coarsely chopped
1 tablespoon olive oil
5 scallions, minced
12 ounces cremini mushrooms, sliced

3 tablespoons dry sherry
1 teaspoon agave nectar or sugar
2 tablespoons freshly squeezed lemon juice
1 teaspoon minced fresh thyme,
   or ½ teaspoon dried
¼ teaspoon freshly ground black pepper

Combine the quinoa and broth in a saucepan and bring to a boil. Add the salt to taste, reduce the heat to medium-low, cover, and simmer until the quinoa is cooked, 15 to 20 minutes. After 10 minutes of cooking, remove the lid, stir the chard into the quinoa, then cover again to finish cooking.

While the quinoa is cooking, heat the oil in a skillet over medium heat. Add the scallions and mushrooms and cook until the mushrooms soften, about 3 minutes. Add the sherry, agave, lemon juice, thyme, pepper, and salt to taste. Cook, stirring, to glaze the mushrooms, about 3 minutes. When ready to serve, spoon the quinoa and chard onto plates or into a large shallow bowl. Top with the mushroom mixture. Serve hot.

sweet and spicy tempeh

serves 4

Fragrant hoisin sauce and a touch of sugar provide the sweet, and fiery sriracha brings the heat in this flavorful tempeh stir-fry that lends itself equally well to seitan or extra-firm tofu. It's great served over rice or quinoa with vegetables on the side; my preference would be to add some steamed broccoli or carrots to the tempeh mixture just before serving, to coat with the sauce. For a sauce that leans to the spicy, use two teaspoons sriracha instead of just one—for a sweeter sauce, go with two teaspoons of sugar rather than one.

1 pound tempeh, cut into 1-inch dice
½ cup canned crushed tomatoes
⅓ cup hoisin sauce
¼ cup soy sauce
3 tablespoons rice vinegar
2 tablespoons orange or pineapple juice
1 to 2 teaspoons light brown sugar

1 to 2 teaspoons sriracha sauce
½ teaspoon salt
2 tablespoons neutral vegetable oil
1 yellow or green bell pepper, diced
3 cloves garlic, minced
4 scallions, minced
1 cup fresh or canned diced pineapple

Steam the tempeh over simmering water for 10 to 15 minutes to mellow the flavor. Set aside and blot dry.

In a bowl, combine the tomatoes, hoisin, soy sauce, vinegar, orange juice, sugar, sriracha, and salt. Mix well and set aside.

Heat the oil in a large skillet over medium-high heat. Add the tempeh and cook until browned, about 5 minutes. Add the bell pepper and cook until softened, about 5 minutes. Add the garlic, scallions, and pineapple and cook until fragrant, 30 seconds. Add the reserved sauce, stirring to coat. Cook to blend the flavors, a few minutes longer. Serve hot.

seitan forestière

serves 4

Here's a quick way to turn sautéed seitan into a special meal. Inspired by the classic forestière sauce, this vegan version features the requisite mushrooms, enriched by a flavorful brown sauce combined with soy creamer. I like to serve it over rice or noodles to catch every bit of the sauce. Accompany it with a green vegetable such as roasted asparagus or sautéed spinach.

2 tablespoons olive oil
¼ pound wild mushrooms, such as porcini, coarsely chopped (2 cups)
¼ pound white mushrooms, coarsely chopped (2 cups)
12 ounces seitan, thinly sliced

½ cup Sienna Sauce (see page 167)
½ cup soy creamer
⅛ teaspoon freshly grated nutmeg
⅛ teaspoon cayenne
Salt and freshly ground black pepper

Heat 1 tablespoon of the oil in a skillet over medium heat. Add the mushrooms and cook until softened, 5 minutes. Cook until all the liquid has evaporated. Transfer all but ½ cup of the mushrooms to a food processor or blender and puree until smooth. Set aside.

In the same skillet, heat the remaining 1 tablespoon oil over medium-high heat. Add the seitan and cook until browned on both sides, about 4 minutes per side. Add all the reserved mushrooms (both pureed and sliced) to the skillet. Stir in the sauce, soy creamer, nutmeg, cayenne, and salt and pepper to taste. Simmer for 5 minutes. Serve hot, with the sauce spooned over the seitan.

tempeh with
mellow mustard sauce

serves 4

Tempeh provides an ideal vehicle for this luscious mustard sauce inspired by Sauce Robert (pronounced ROH-bare), a classic brown mustard sauce known as one of the "small" or compound sauces in French cooking. Serve over freshly cooked rice or quinoa or wide egg-free noodles.

1 tablespoon olive oil
12 ounces tempeh, cut into thin slices
¼ cup minced yellow onion
½ cup dry white wine

2 tablespoons Dijon mustard
1 cup Sienna Sauce (see page 167)
2 tablespoons minced fresh parsley

Heat the oil in a large skillet over medium heat. Add the tempeh and onion and cook until the onion is softened and the tempeh is browned, about 8 minutes. Add the wine and bring to a boil until it is reduced by half, 5 minutes. Reduce the heat to low. Add the mustard to the sauce and stir to combine. Stir the sauce mixture into the tempeh and simmer until hot, 5 minutes. Taste and adjust the seasonings. Remove from the heat and stir in the parsley. Serve hot, spooning the extra sauce over the tempeh.

pasta express

Pasta has long been a go-to choice for a quick meal that everyone enjoys. After all, once the water comes to a boil, pasta is ready in just a few minutes. Not only is pasta easy to make, it's economical too. However, many times we fall into a pasta rut, saucing it the same way every time. That's where this chapter can help. The variety of flavors and ingredients used in these recipes can transform pasta night from "same old" to "sensational."

Dazzle your taste buds with Orecchiette with Puttanesca Pesto; Penne with Artichokes, Walnuts, and Olives; or Ziti with Brasciole-Inspired Tomato Sauce.

Indulge in the healthful decadence of Rotini with Creamy Avocado–Herb Sauce. Enjoy lasagne without turning on the oven with the amazing Skillet Lasagne. Savor a taste of the East with Spicy Peanut–Hoisin Noodles with Tofu and Broccoli or Curried Cavatappi with Chickpeas and Chutney. Tapping into a world of flavors, these diverse pasta and noodle dishes are sure to satisfy your family and friends.

one-pot pasta primavera

serves 4

I love to cook, but I hate the cleanup. That's why I like this recipe with only one pot to wash. The vegetables cook right with the pasta, then get added back into the same pot to mingle with the delectable sauce.

12 ounces penne or other bite-size pasta
1 carrot, thinly sliced
2 cups small broccoli florets
1 small zucchini, halved lengthwise and
    cut into ¼-inch slices
3 tablespoons olive oil, plus more for
    drizzling

5 cloves garlic, minced
4 scallions, minced
¼ cup dry white wine or vegetable broth
1½ cups grape tomatoes, halved
¼ cup fresh basil leaves
Salt and freshly ground black pepper

Cook the penne in a large pot of boiling salted water until just tender, about 10 minutes. About 3 minutes before the pasta is done cooking, add the carrot, broccoli, and zucchini to the pasta pot. Drain the pasta and vegetables well and set aside. Return the pot to the stove. Add the 3 tablespoons oil and heat over medium heat. Add the garlic and scallions and cook until softened, 1 minute. Add the wine and cook for 30 seconds. Return the pasta and vegetables to the pot. Add the tomatoes, basil, and salt and pepper to taste. Cook, tossing gently to combine, and heat through. Taste and adjust the seasonings. Drizzle on a little more olive oil, if desired.

note: To make this or any of the other pasta recipes gluten free, use a gluten-free pasta.

penne with artichokes, walnuts, and olives

serves 4

This is one great pasta dish, loaded with flavors and textures. I especially like the way the walnuts play off the olives, artichokes, and sun-dried tomatoes. Instead of canned artichoke hearts, you could substitute 1½ cups of drained marinated artichoke hearts or cooked frozen artichoke hearts.

12 ounces penne or other bite-size pasta
2 tablespoons olive oil
5 cloves garlic, minced
½ cup chopped walnut pieces
1 (14-ounce) can artichoke hearts, drained, rinsed, and coarsely chopped
½ cup pitted kalamata olives, halved
⅓ cup oil-packed sun-dried tomatoes, cut into thin strips
½ teaspoon salt
½ teaspoon red pepper flakes
¼ teaspoon freshly ground black pepper
3 tablespoons dry white wine
½ cup vegetable broth or pasta cooking water
2 tablespoons minced fresh parsley or basil

Cook the penne in a large pot of boiling salted water until just tender, about 10 minutes. While the pasta is cooking, heat the oil in a skillet over medium heat. Add the garlic and cook until fragrant, about 1 minute. Stir in the walnuts, then add the artichokes, olives, sun-dried tomatoes, salt, red pepper flakes, black pepper, and wine. Add the broth and simmer to heat through and blend the flavors, 1 to 2 minutes. Drain the cooked pasta and return to the pot. Add the artichoke mixture and toss gently to combine. Taste and adjust the seasonings. Drizzle on a little more olive oil, if desired. Serve hot, garnished with parsley.

rotini with 10-minute tomato–olive sauce

serves 4

Sure, you could just reach for a jar of prepared sauce, but this sauce may entice you to make your own. Ready by the time the pasta is done cooking, the lusty sauce is made with three kinds of tomatoes, lots of garlic, kalamata olives, and fresh herbs. You won't find all that in a jarred sauce.

12 ounces rotini
1 tablespoon olive oil
5 cloves garlic, minced
1 (28-ounce) can crushed tomatoes
1 (14.5-ounce) can diced tomatoes, drained
¾ cup pitted kalamata olives, halved
¼ cup oil-packed sun-dried tomatoes, minced

2 tablespoons minced fresh parsley
¼ cup chopped fresh basil leaves
½ teaspoon salt
¼ teaspoon red pepper flakes
Freshly ground black pepper

Cook the rotini in a large pot of boiling salted water until just tender, about 10 minutes. While the pasta is cooking, heat the oil in a saucepan over medium heat. Add the garlic and cook until fragrant, 1 minute. Stir in the crushed tomatoes and diced tomatoes, and simmer until the tomatoes have broken down a bit, 5 minutes. Add the olives, sun-dried tomatoes, parsley, basil, salt, red pepper flakes, and black pepper to taste. Cook to blend flavors, stirring occasionally, about 4 minutes longer. Drain the cooked pasta well and serve topped with the sauce.

ziti with roasted cauliflower and tomatoes

serves 4

Roasted cauliflower has such a tremendous flavor, I thought it deserved to be the star of the show rather than a side dish. Cherry tomatoes add color and their special sweetness, while garlic, pine nuts, raisins, and capers lend a Sicilian aura to the dish.

1 small head cauliflower
½ cups cherry tomatoes
2 tablespoons olive oil, plus more for drizzling
Salt and freshly ground black pepper
12 ounces ziti or other bite-size pasta
4 cloves garlic, minced
¼ cup pine nuts

¼ cup raisins
2 tablespoons capers
¼ teaspoon red pepper flakes
¼ teaspoon ground fennel seed
½ cup vegetable broth, white wine, or pasta water
3 tablespoons chopped fresh basil or parsley

Preheat the oven to 425°F. Oil a baking sheet and set aside. Use a sharp knife to remove the core from the head of the cauliflower. Place the cauliflower on a work surface, cored side down. Use a large serrated knife to cut the cauliflower into ½-inch slices (as you would slice a loaf of bread). Break the cauliflower slices into bite-size pieces and arrange on the prepared baking sheet. Arrange the cherry tomatoes among the cauliflower pieces, drizzle with 1 tablespoon of the olive oil, and season to taste with salt and pepper. Roast the cauliflower and tomatoes, turning once, about halfway through, until the cauliflower is tender, about 15 minutes.

While the cauliflower and tomatoes are roasting, cook the ziti in a large pot of boiling salted water until just tender, about 10 minutes.

In a small skillet, heat the remaining 1 tablespoon oil over medium heat. Add the garlic and pine nuts and cook to soften the garlic and lightly toast the pine nuts, about 1 minute. Stir in the raisins, capers, red pepper flakes, and fennel. Add the broth and season to taste with salt and pepper. Simmer to blend flavors, 1 minute. Remove from the heat.

Drain the cooked pasta well and return to the pot. Add the garlic mixture and the cauliflower and tomatoes and toss gently to combine. Taste and adjust the seasonings and drizzle with a little more olive oil, if desired. Garnish with the basil and serve immediately.

linguine with artichoke and white bean alfredo

serves 4

Piquant artichokes punctuate the creamy white bean sauce in this luscious interpretation of the classic Alfredo dish. To get the sauce perfectly smooth, use a Vitamix or other high-speed blender. Otherwise, the sauce may retain bits of artichoke, which is okay, too.

12 ounces linguine

3 cloves garlic, crushed

½ teaspoon salt

1 (9-ounce) jar marinated artichokes, drained

1 cup home-cooked white beans, or canned beans, drained and rinsed

1 tablespoon nutritional yeast

2 tablespoons olive oil

½ cup hot pasta water or vegetable broth

½ cup soy creamer (optional)

2 tablespoons minced fresh parsley

Cook the linguine in a large pot of boiling salted water until just tender, about 10 minutes. While the pasta is cooking, combine the garlic and salt in a blender or food processor and mince well. Add the artichokes, white beans, nutritional yeast, olive oil, and hot pasta water and blend until smooth and creamy. Add the soy creamer, if using, and blend until smooth. Taste and adjust the seasonings. Drain the pasta well and return it to the pot. Add the sauce and toss to combine. Serve hot, garnished with the parsley.

summer pasta with red and yellow tomatoes

serves 4

Inspired by my own garden-fresh vegetables, this lovely pasta dish makes regular appearances in my house during the summer, when tomatoes, summer squash, and basil are at their peak. Creamy cannellini beans add protein and substance. To add to the summer theme, I use farfalle (butterfly) pasta, but any bite-size pasta shape can be used.

12 ounces farfalle or other bite-size pasta
2 tablespoons olive oil, plus more for drizzling
5 cloves garlic, minced
5 scallions, minced
2 small zucchini, thinly sliced
1 small yellow squash, thinly sliced

4 cups fresh baby spinach leaves
Salt and freshly ground black pepper
1½ cups red grape tomatoes, halved
1½ cups yellow grape tomatoes, halved
1½ cups home-cooked cannellini beans, or 1 (15-ounce) can, drained and rinsed
½ cup fresh basil leaves, torn

Cook the farfalle in a large pot of boiling salted water until just tender, about 10 minutes. While the pasta is cooking, heat the 2 tablespoons oil in a large skillet over medium heat. Add the garlic, scallions, zucchini, and yellow squash and cook until the squash is softened, stirring frequently, 5 to 7 minutes. Add the spinach and cook, stirring, until wilted, 2 minutes. Season to taste with salt and pepper.

Drain the cooked pasta and return to the pot. Add the squash mixture, the red and yellow tomatoes, beans, and basil. Season to taste with salt and pepper, then toss gently to combine. Serve immediately, drizzled with a little more olive oil, if desired.

ziti with brasciole-inspired tomato sauce

serves 4

This Sicilian-style pasta dish was inspired by my mother's brasciole recipe which contained lots of garlic, parsley, and raisins for a zesty and deliciously different tomato-based sauce. If anyone in your family is averse to raisins in a savory dish, you can leave them out.

12 ounces ziti or other bite-size pasta
1 tablespoon olive oil
5 cloves garlic, minced
1 (28-ounce) can crushed tomatoes
1 (14-ounce) can diced tomatoes, well
    drained
¼ cup golden raisins
¾ teaspoon salt

½ teaspoon dried oregano
½ teaspoon ground fennel seed
½ teaspoon red pepper flakes
½ teaspoon sugar
¼ teaspoon freshly ground black pepper
¼ cup toasted panko or other bread
    crumbs
¼ cup minced fresh parsley

Cook the ziti in a large pot of boiling salted water until just tender, about 10 minutes. While the pasta is cooking, heat the oil in a saucepan over medium heat. Add the garlic and cook until fragrant, 1 minute. Stir in the crushed tomatoes, diced tomatoes, raisins, salt, oregano, fennel, red pepper flakes, sugar, and black pepper. Cook, stirring occasionally, for 10 minutes until the sauce is hot and the flavors are well blended.

Drain the cooked pasta well and return to the pot. Add the sauce and toss to combine. Serve hot topped with the bread crumbs and parsley.

rotini with creamy avocado–herb sauce

serves 4

Luxuriously creamy and delicious, this sauce is also simple to make. If you don't have a high-speed blender, you might want to soak the cashews in water for several hours or overnight to soften them for a smoother sauce. I like to make this with springy rotini, but any small pasta shape is fine.

12 ounces rotini or other bite-size pasta
½ cup cashews
3 cloves garlic
½ teaspoon salt
½ cup fresh basil leaves
¼ cup fresh parsley leaves
1 tablespoon snipped fresh chives

1 teaspoon fresh thyme leaves
¼ teaspoon freshly ground black pepper
2 ripe avocados
2 tablespoons freshly squeezed lemon juice
¾ to 1 cup vegetable broth
2 tablespoons olive oil

Cook the rotini in a large pot of boiling salted water until just tender, about 10 minutes. While the pasta is cooking, combine the cashews, garlic, and salt in a blender or food processor and process until finely ground. Add the basil, parsley, chives, thyme, and pepper and pulse to chop well. Halve and pit the avocados, spoon out the flesh, and chop. Add the avocados, lemon juice, broth, and olive oil and process until smooth and creamy. Add a little more broth if the sauce is too thick. Taste and adjust the seasonings. Drain the cooked pasta and return to the pot. Add the sauce and toss to combine. Serve immediately.

note: Try to eat the sauce immediately as it will begin to turn brown if made in advance—a good excuse not to have any leftovers!

linguine with cannellini pesto

serves 4

Lots of basil and garlic and a little miso or nutritional yeast combine with cannellini beans for a satisfying pesto that is lower in fat and higher in protein than a typical pesto, without sacrificing any of the great flavor. The pesto can also be stirred into vinaigrette or minestrone for added flavor. It's also good mixed with vegan mayonnaise to spread on a roasted vegetable sandwich. Another pasta may be used instead of the linguine, if desired.

12 ounces linguine
5 cloves garlic, crushed
½ teaspoon salt
1 cup home-cooked cannellini beans, or
   canned beans, drained and rinsed

1 tablespoon white miso paste or
   nutritional yeast
1½ cups fresh basil leaves
2 tablespoons olive oil
½ cup hot pasta water

Cook the linguine in a large pot of boiling salted water until just tender, about 10 minutes. While the pasta is cooking, combine the garlic and salt in a blender or food processor and process until finely minced. Add the beans, miso, basil, and oil and process until smooth. Add as much of the hot pasta water as needed to reach the desired consistency. Drain the cooked pasta and return to the pot. Add the pesto and toss to combine. Taste and adjust the seasoning, adding more salt if needed. Serve hot.

orecchiette with puttanesca pesto

serves 4

It's no secret that puttanesca sauce is my favorite way to enjoy pasta. But I also like pesto. With this lush puttanesca pesto, now I can enjoy them both at the same time, and in the time it takes to cook the pasta, the pesto is finished and the food processor is cleaned. If orecchiette (little ears) are unavailable, use your favorite pasta instead. For a saucier pesto, add up to ½ cup of the hot pasta water to the pesto after processing.

12 ounces orrechiette
5 cloves garlic
½ cup pitted kalamata olives
⅓ cup pitted green olives
1 fresh ripe tomato, coarsely chopped
¼ cup oil-packed sun-dried tomatoes

¼ cup chopped fresh parsley
¼ cup fresh basil leaves
2 tablespoons capers
2 tablespoons olive oil
Salt and freshly ground black pepper

Cook the orecchiette in a large pot of boiling salted water until just tender, about 10 minutes. While the pasta is cooking, place the garlic in a blender or food processor and process until finely minced. Add the kalamata olives, green olives, fresh tomatoes, sun-dried tomatoes, parsley, basil, capers, and oil and process until smooth. Season to taste with salt and pepper. Drain the cooked pasta and return to the pot. Add the pesto and toss to combine. Serve hot.

note: This flavorful pesto can be used beyond pasta: try it on baked potatoes, mixed into cooked couscous or rice, spread on a baguette, added to scrambled tofu, baked in puff pastry, to name just a few. I have it on good authority that it can also be mixed into mashed avocado and used as a dip for olive and caper tortilla chips.

skillet lasagne

serves 4 to 6

This is a quick way to get lasagne on the table without having to heat up the oven. I usually take the extra step of softening the noodles a bit in some boiling water. While that step isn't absolutely necessary, you may need to cook the lasagne a few minutes longer if you omit it. When Linda Evans tested this recipe, she admits she was skeptical and was pleasantly surprised how well the noodles cooked this way and how easy it was to make. The optional kalamata olives add flavor and texture to the filling.

8 ounces lasagna noodles broken into
   thirds
1 pound firm tofu, drained
3 tablespoons nutritional yeast
1 tablespoon freshly squeezed lemon juice
½ teaspoon garlic powder
½ teaspoon onion powder
½ teaspoon dried basil
½ teaspoon dried oregano

Salt and freshly ground black pepper
3 tablespoons minced fresh parsley
⅓ cup pitted kalamata olives, chopped
   (optional)
½ cup water
3 cups marinara sauce, bottled or
   homemade
Vegan Parmesan or mozzarella cheese
   (optional)

Place the lasagna noodles in a shallow heatproof container and cover with boiling water. Set aside while you make the filling.

Mash the tofu in a bowl. Add the nutritional yeast, lemon juice, garlic powder, onion powder, basil, oregano, ½ teaspoon salt, ¼ teaspoon pepper, parsley, and olives, if using. Mix well and set aside.

Heat a large nonstick skillet over medium heat. Add the water and 1 cup of the marinara sauce, stirring to blend. Remove the lasagna noodles from the hot water and arrange half of them on top of the sauce. Top with the reserved tofu mixture, then top with the remaining noodles. Pour the remaining marinara sauce over the noodles. Cover and bring to a simmer. Reduce the heat to medium-low and cook until the noodles are tender, 15 to 20 minutes. Remove the lid and top with the vegan cheese, if using. Remove from the heat and let stand, covered, until the lasagne is set and the cheese is melted, 5 minutes. Serve immediately.

southwestern pasta toss

serves 4

Pasta, pinto beans, and corn join forces with the flavors of the Southwest in this quick and delicious meal. Grape tomatoes, cilantro, and avocado add color and refreshing flavors. If you prefer a saucy pasta, stir in ½ cup of salsa a few minutes before serving. Or, you could drizzle on a little olive oil when ready to serve.

12 ounces rotini or other bite-size pasta
1 ripe avocado
1 tablespoon olive oil
5 scallions, minced
3 cloves garlic, minced
1 serrano chile, seeded and minced
   (optional)
1½ cups home-cooked pinto beans, or
   1 (15-ounce) can, drained and rinsed

1 cup cooked fresh or frozen corn kernels
¼ cup canned chopped mild green chiles,
   drained
½ teaspoon chili powder
½ teaspoon ground cumin
½ teaspoon salt
Freshly ground black pepper
1 cup grape tomatoes, halved
3 tablespoons chopped fresh cilantro

Cook the rotini in a large pot of boiling salted water until just tender, about 10 minutes. While the pasta is cooking, halve and pit the avocado, spoon out the flesh, and chop. Set aside. Heat the oil in a skillet over medium heat. Add the scallions, garlic, and serrano chile, if using, and cook until softened, about 1 minute. Stir in the beans, corn, mild chiles, chili powder, cumin, salt, and pepper to taste. Cook until the flavors are blended, 5 minutes. Add the tomatoes and cilantro and stir to combine. Drain the cooked pasta and return to the pot. Add the bean and vegetable mixture and toss to combine. Serve immediately topped with the reserved avocado.

farfalle with sesame cabbage

serves 4

Tahini, sesame oil, and soy sauce add a flavorful nuance to this reimagining of halushki, a favorite comfort food dish I enjoyed as a child. The original version contained little more than meltingly soft cabbage and onions combined with chewy pasta. I think this new interpretation takes it to the next level.

12 ounces farfalle or other bite-size pasta
1 tablespoon neutral vegetable oil
1 (10-ounce) bag shredded cabbage
  (4 packed cups)
2 carrots, shredded
5 scallions, minced
2 cloves garlic, minced
¼ cup tahini

2 tablespoons soy sauce
2 tablespoons freshly squeezed lemon juice
1 teaspoon toasted sesame oil
1 cup hot pasta water
Salt and freshly ground black pepper
2 tablespoons toasted sesame seeds
3 tablespoons chopped fresh parsley

Cook the farfalle in a large pot of boiling salted water until just tender, about 10 minutes. While the pasta is cooking, heat the oil in a skillet over medium heat. Add the cabbage and carrots. Cover and cook until softened, 5 to 7 minutes. Stir in the scallions and garlic and cook, stirring occasionally, until softened, 3 minutes longer.

In a bowl, combine the tahini, soy sauce, lemon juice, sesame oil, and pasta water. Stir to blend. Add the sauce to the cabbage mixture, tossing to coat. Drain the cooked pasta, then return it to the pot. Add the cabbage mixture and toss to combine. Season to taste with salt and pepper. Serve hot, sprinkled with sesame seeds and parsley.

curried cavatappi with chickpeas and chutney

serves 4 to 6

One doesn't usually think of pasta and curry in the same dish. After you try this recipe, you may wonder why you didn't think of it sooner. Coconut milk combines with chutney for a rich creamy sauce that can be hot or mild, depending on the spiciness of the chutney you use. A savory (not sweet) chutney works best in this dish.

12 ounces cavatappi or other bite-size pasta
1 tablespoon neutral vegetable oil
1 small yellow onion, minced
1 small carrot, thinly sliced
2 tablespoons curry powder, hot or mild
1 teaspoon ground coriander
½ teaspoon ground cumin

1½ cups home-cooked chickpeas, or 1 (15-ounce) can, drained and rinsed
½ cup frozen peas, partially thawed
1 (13-ounce) can unsweetened coconut milk
⅓ cup chutney, hot or mild (not sweet)
3 tablespoons minced fresh cilantro or parsley

Cook the cavatappi in a large pot of boiling salted water until just tender, about 10 minutes. While the pasta is cooking, heat the oil in a skillet over medium heat. Add the onion and carrot. Cover and cook until softened, about 5 minutes. Stir in the curry powder, coriander, and cumin. Add the chickpeas, peas, and coconut milk. Simmer until hot and the flavors have blended, 3 minutes. Stir in the chutney and keep warm over low heat.

Drain the cooked pasta and return to the pot. Add the reserved chickpea mixture and toss to combine. Serve hot topped with the cilantro.

spicy peanut–hoisin noodles with tofu and broccoli

serves 4

The sauce for this flavorful noodle dish is so delicious you may want to eat it with a spoon. But you'll be glad if you wait and toss it with the other ingredients and serve it for a fast and fantastic one-dish meal.

12 ounces linguine

¼ cup creamy peanut butter

2 tablespoon hoisin sauce

2 tablespoons soy sauce

2 tablespoons rice vinegar

1 tablespoon sriracha sauce

1 tablespoon agave nectar or maple syrup

1 teaspoon toasted sesame oil

1 cup vegetable broth

1 tablespoon neutral vegetable oil

1 pound extra-firm tofu, drained and diced

Salt and freshly ground black pepper

3 scallions, minced

2 cloves garlic, minced

1 teaspoon grated fresh ginger

3 cups small broccoli florets

1 carrot, thinly sliced

2 tablespoons chopped peanuts

Cook the linguine in a large pot of boiling salted water until just tender, about 10 minutes. While the pasta is cooking, in a small saucepan, combine the peanut butter, hoisin sauce, soy sauce, rice vinegar, sriracha, agave, and sesame oil, stirring to blend. Stir in as much of the broth as needed to make a smooth sauce. Keep warm over very low heat.

Heat the oil in a large skillet over medium-high heat. Add the tofu and cook until golden brown all over, 8 to 10 minutes. Season to taste with salt and pepper. Add the scallions, garlic, and ginger, and cook until softened, about 1 minute.

About 3 minutes before the pasta is cooked, add the broccoli and carrot to the pasta water. Drain the cooked pasta and vegetables and return them to the pot. Stir in the tofu and the reserved sauce and toss gently to combine. Serve hot sprinkled with the peanuts.

primavera-style coconut-cashew noodles

serves 4

Colorful vegetables and chewy noodles merge deliciously in a creamy and fragrant sauce. Use Thai basil if at all possible, although cilantro or regular basil can be used if necessary. Instead of cashew butter, you can substitute peanut butter or a Thai curry paste (red or green are both good here) for different flavor sensations. Add some sautéed tofu or tempeh for extra protein, and swap out the veggies according to your preference or what's on hand.

12 ounces linguine
1 tablespoon neutral vegetable oil
5 scallions, minced
1 carrot, shredded
1 teaspoon grated fresh ginger
1 cup snow peas
⅓ cup fresh Thai basil, cilantro,
   or regular basil

2 tablespoons cashew butter
1 tablespoon sriracha sauce
1 tablespoon soy sauce
1 teaspoon light brown sugar
1 (13-ounce) can unsweetened
   coconut milk

Cook the linguine in a large pot of boiling salted water until just tender, about 10 minutes. While the pasta is cooking, heat the oil in a large skillet over medium heat. Add the scallions, carrot, ginger, and snow peas and cook until the snow peas are softened, 2 to 3 minutes. Add the basil and cook, stirring gently, until hot.

In a small bowl, combine the cashew butter, sriracha, soy sauce, and sugar. Stir in the coconut milk until well blended. Stir the mixture into the vegetables and keep warm. Drain the cooked pasta and return to the pot. Add the sauce and vegetable mixture and toss to combine. Serve hot.

soups
in
short order

Soup is often associated with long-simmering kettles on the stove. While that may be true sometimes, the recipes in this chapter are here to prove that's not always the case. From a rich and colorful Moroccan-Spiced Pumpkin Soup to a zesty Tomato Tortilla Soup, these flavorful recipes can be on the table in 30 minutes. That's not to say that, like most soups, these don't taste even better when reheated the next day, because they do.

Choices abound with hearty soups like White Bean and Basil Soup or Island Black Bean Soup with Quick Mango Salsa, and creamy vegetable soups like Roasted Asparagus Soup or a Cream of Mushroom Soup that is miles away from the gloppy canned stuff. There's even a spicy Asian Noodle Soup with Bok Choy and Shiitakes and a gorgeous Chard and Red Lentil Soup. Many of these soups are satisfying enough to be meals in themselves.

A recipe for homemade vegetable broth can be found on page 13. Otherwise, you can use a commercially prepared broth or make a quick broth using a vegetable base and water. Because different broths have varying degrees of saltiness, it's best to add salt to taste in these recipes.

quick vegetable and quinoa soup

serves 4

Think of this soup next time you want a soul-satisfying vegetable soup that's ready in just 30 minutes. The vegetables and beans can be varied according to what you have on hand.

1 tablespoon olive oil
1 yellow onion, minced
1 carrot, thinly sliced
2 cloves garlic, minced
⅔ cup quinoa, well rinsed
6 cups vegetable broth
1½ cups home-cooked dark red kidney beans, or 1 (15-ounce) can, drained and rinsed

1 (14.5-ounce) can diced fire-roasted tomatoes, undrained
1 small zucchini, chopped
1 cup fresh or frozen corn kernels
Salt
½ teaspoon dried basil
½ teaspoon dried marjoram
¼ teaspoon freshly ground black pepper
3 cups chopped baby spinach
2 tablespoons minced fresh parsley

Heat the oil in a large pot over medium heat. Add the onion, carrot, and garlic. Cover and cook for 5 minutes to soften. Stir in the quinoa, then add the broth, beans, tomatoes, zucchini, corn, 1 teaspoon salt or to taste, the basil, marjoram, and pepper. Bring to a boil, then reduce to a simmer and cook until the vegetables and quinoa are tender, about 20 minutes. Stir in the spinach and parsley and cook until the spinach is wilted, 1 to 2 minutes. Taste and adjust the seasonings. Serve hot.

white bean and basil soup

serves 4

Fragrant basil and creamy white beans star in this light and lovely soup. I like to use cannellini beans in this soup—I think they have more flavor than other white beans. For a heartier soup, stir in some cooked elbow macaroni and tomato sauce about 5 minutes before serving.

1 tablespoon olive oil
1 large yellow onion, minced
1 carrot, minced
1 celery rib, minced
3 to 5 cloves garlic, minced
1 teaspoon dried basil
3 cups home-cooked white beans, or
  2 (15-ounce) cans, drained and rinsed

6 cups vegetable broth
2 tablespoons thinly sliced sun-dried
  tomatoes, oil-packed or reconstituted
  dry-packed
Salt and freshly ground black pepper
½ cup torn fresh basil leaves

Heat the oil in a large pot over medium heat. Add the onion, carrot, celery, and garlic. Cover and cook until softened, 5 minutes. Stir in the dried basil, then add the beans, broth, tomatoes, and salt and pepper to taste. Bring to a boil then reduce the heat to medium and simmer until the vegetables are tender, about 15 minutes. Stir in the fresh basil and serve hot.

cream of mushroom soup

serves 4

Unlike the canned version, this cream of mushroom soup tastes fresh and vibrant. Smoked paprika, dill, and dry sherry contribute to the depth of flavor while vegan sour cream adds richness.

1 tablespoon olive oil
1 yellow onion, minced
1 celery rib, minced
1 pound white mushrooms, thinly sliced
3 tablespoons all-purpose flour
2 teaspoons smoked paprika
2 teaspoons dried dill
1 tablespoon dry sherry or soy sauce

4 cups vegetable broth
1 cup unsweetened nondairy milk
1 teaspoon salt
¼ teaspoon freshly ground black pepper
2 teaspoons freshly squeezed lemon juice
2 tablespoons chopped fresh parsley
¼ cup vegan sour cream

Heat the oil in a large pot over medium heat. Add the onion and celery. Cover and cook until softened, 5 minutes. Add the mushrooms and cook until softened, about 4 minutes. Sprinkle on the flour and paprika, stirring to coat the vegetables, and cook out the raw taste from the flour, about 3 minutes. Add the dill and sherry, then slowly add the broth while stirring to thicken slightly. Simmer until the flavors are blended, 10 minutes. Stir in the nondairy milk, 1 teaspoon salt or to taste, the pepper, lemon juice, and 1 tablespoon of the parsley.

Use an immersion blender to puree half of the soup in the pot. Or, puree half of the soup in a stand blender or food processor and return to the pot to heat through.

Serve hot in soup bowls, and top each serving with a spoonful of sour cream and a sprinkling of the remaining parsley.

tomato tortilla soup

serves 4

Crunchy tortilla strips feature prominently in this spicy soup, while avocado provides a cool and creamy contrast. Recipe testers loved this soup: "Nice and spicy. A real winner. Delicious!" Talk about rave reviews! Variation: For a heartier, more stewlike dish, and to cut the heat, stir in 1 to 2 cups of cooked rice near the end of the cooking time. To cut the heat further, serve vegan sour cream on the side.

2 (7-inch) corn or flour tortillas, cut into ¼-inch strips
1½ tablespoons olive oil
1 ripe avocado
1 yellow onion, finely chopped
2 cloves garlic, minced
2 (14.5-ounce) cans diced tomatoes with green chiles, including juice
1 cup tomato salsa, hot or mild

1½ cups home-cooked dark red kidney beans, or 1 (15-ounce) can, drained and rinsed
1 cup fresh or frozen corn kernels
1½ teaspoons chili powder
½ teaspoon ground cumin
½ teaspoon smoked paprika
3 cups vegetable broth
Salt and freshly ground black pepper
3 tablespoons chopped fresh cilantro

Preheat the oven to 400°F. Oil a baking sheet. Toss the tortilla strips and 1 tablespoon of the oil in a bowl to coat the tortillas. Spread the tortilla strips on the prepared baking sheet and bake until crisp, turning once, about 4 minutes per side. Remove from the oven and set aside. Halve and pit the avocado, spoon out the flesh, and dice. Set aside.

Heat the remaining ½ tablespoon oil in a large pot. Add the onion and garlic, cover, and cook until softened, 5 minutes. Add the tomatoes, salsa, kidney beans, corn, chili powder, cumin, and paprika. Stir in the vegetable broth and season to taste with salt and pepper. Bring to a boil, then reduce the heat to medium and simmer to blend the flavors, 10 to 15 minutes. Stir in the cilantro. Ladle the soup into bowls and serve hot topped with the reserved tortilla strips and avocado.

sweet potato–spinach soup

serves 4

The only thing more enticing than the vibrant colors of this soup is its luscious flavor. Peanut butter enriches the delicious broth that complements the sweet potato, spinach, and tomatoes. A garnish of chopped peanuts adds a wonderful crunch.

2 teaspoons neutral vegetable oil
1 yellow onion, finely chopped
1 large sweet potato, diced
1 tablespoon grated fresh ginger
2 teaspoons ground coriander
¼ teaspoon cayenne
1 (14-ounce) can diced tomatoes, drained

2 tablespoons soy sauce
⅓ cup creamy peanut butter
4 cups vegetable broth
Salt and freshly ground black pepper
1½ cups unsweetened nondairy milk
4 cups fresh baby spinach
¼ cup chopped peanuts

Heat the oil in a large pot over medium heat. Add the onion and sweet potato. Cover and cook until softened, 5 minutes. Stir in the ginger, coriander, and ¼ teaspoon cayenne or to taste. Add the tomatoes and soy sauce.

In a small bowl, combine the peanut butter with 1 cup of the broth, stirring until smooth. Stir the peanut butter mixture into the soup, then add the remaining broth and season to taste with salt and pepper. Bring to a boil, reduce the heat to low, and simmer until the vegetables are tender, 10 to 15 minutes.

Stir in the nondairy milk and spinach and cook until the spinach is wilted, about 3 minutes. Serve hot, sprinkled with the chopped peanuts.

island black bean soup
with quick mango salsa

serves 4

I never tasted a black bean soup I didn't like, but this one is an all-time favorite thanks to the addition of mango salsa which provides a delicious flavor counterpoint and a gorgeous color accent to the soup.

2 teaspoons olive oil
1 red onion, finely chopped
3 cloves garlic, minced
3 cups home-cooked black beans, or
   2 (15-ounce) cans, drained and rinsed
1 (14-ounce) can diced tomatoes with
   chiles, including juice
1 teaspoon ground cumin

½ teaspoon ground coriander
3 cups vegetable broth
Salt and freshly ground black pepper
1 fresh ripe mango
3 tablespoons minced fresh cilantro
1 tablespoon freshly squeezed lime juice

Heat the oil in a large pot over medium heat. Add all but 2 tablespoons of the onion and cook until softened, about 5 minutes. Add the garlic and cook until softened, 1 minute longer. Stir in the beans, tomatoes, cumin, coriander, vegetable broth, and salt and pepper to taste. Bring to a boil, then reduce the heat to medium and simmer until the flavors are blended, about 15 minutes.

While the soup is simmering, slice through the mango lengthwise, next to one side of the flat pit, and detach; repeat for the other side. Spoon out the flesh, chop, and transfer to a bowl. Add the reserved 2 tablespoons onion, the cilantro, and lime juice. Mix well and set aside.

When ready to serve, ladle the soup into bowls and top with a spoonful of the salsa.

coconut corn chowder

serves 4 to 6

This sensational chowder has an amazing depth of flavor, especially when you consider that it takes less than 30 minutes to prepare and can be made mostly from pantry ingredients. If you prefer a creamy soup over a chowder, you can puree this chowder with an immersion blender or in a stand blender or food processor if you like.

2 teaspoons olive oil
1 small yellow onion, chopped
2 teaspoons grated fresh ginger
1 russet potato, chopped
1 (14-ounce) can diced tomatoes with
    chiles, drained
3 cups vegetable broth

3 cups fresh or frozen corn kernels
Salt and freshly ground black pepper
1 (13-ounce) can unsweetened coconut milk
3 tablespoons chopped fresh Thai basil or
    cilantro
Sriracha or other hot sauce (optional)

Heat the oil in a large pot over medium-high heat. Add the onion, cover, and cook until softened, about 5 minutes. Stir in the ginger, then add the potato, tomatoes, and vegetable broth and bring to a boil. Reduce the heat to medium, add the corn, and season to taste with salt and pepper. Simmer until the vegetables are tender, about 15 minutes. Stir in the coconut milk and basil. To serve, ladle into bowls and drizzle a small amount of sriracha on top of each bowl if desired.

roasted asparagus soup

serves 4

Ever since I began roasting asparagus several years ago, I rarely cook it any other way. So it's only natural that I'd want to infuse that special roasted flavor into my asparagus soup. To speed things along, get the asparagus roasting and then prepare the rest of the soup while the asparagus cooks. This soup is also good made with roasted cauliflower.

1 pound thin asparagus, cut into 2-inch
   pieces
4 to 5 shallots, thinly sliced
1½ tablespoons olive oil
Salt and freshly ground black pepper

3 cloves garlic, minced
1 Yukon gold potato, shredded
3 cups vegetable broth
1 cup unsweetened nondairy milk
3 tablespoons minced fresh parsley

Preheat the oven to 425°F. Oil a baking sheet. Spread the asparagus and shallots on the prepared baking sheet. Drizzle with ½ tablespoon of the oil and season to taste with salt and pepper. Roast until tender, 8 to 10 minutes. Remove 4 asparagus tips for garnish and reserve.

Heat the remaining 1 tablespoon oil in a large pot over medium heat. Add the garlic and potato. Season to taste with salt and pepper, cover, and cook until softened, 5 minutes. Add the broth and bring to a boil. Reduce the heat to medium, add the roasted asparagus and shallots, and simmer until the vegetables are tender, about 10 minutes.

Remove from the heat and puree the soup with an immersion blender. Or, transfer to a stand blender or food processor and puree in batches, then return to the pot. Stir in the nondairy milk and heat until hot. Taste and adjust the seasonings. Serve sprinkled with the parsley and the reserved asparagus tips.

creamy greens soup

serves 4

Inspired by a Southeast Asian side dish made with spinach and coconut milk, this easy and healthful soup makes a delicious first course or accompaniment to a sandwich or other hearty fare. If you're a member of a CSA (Community Supported Agriculture), then you're probably always looking for new ways to enjoy the abundant greens that are often part of the bounty. To make it more substantial on its own, stir in some cooked quinoa and white beans a few minutes before serving time.

1 tablespoon olive oil
1 small yellow onion, finely chopped
2 cloves garlic, minced
5 cups coarsely chopped greens, such as spinach, chard, kale, or a combination (9 ounces)

2 cups vegetable broth
Salt and freshly ground black pepper
1 (13-ounce) can unsweetened coconut milk, or 1½ cups nondairy milk

Heat the oil in a large pot over medium heat. Add the onion and garlic, cover, and cook until softened, 5 minutes. Add the greens, stirring to wilt, about 3 minutes. Stir in the broth and season to taste with salt and pepper. Bring to a boil, then reduce the heat to medium and simmer until the vegetables are soft and the flavors are well combined, about 10 minutes.

Remove from the heat and puree with an immersion blender. Or, transfer to a stand blender or food processor and puree in batches, then return to the pot. Stir in the coconut milk and heat until hot. Taste and adjust the seasonings.

curried cauliflower soup with roasted cauliflower "rice"

serves 4

Cauliflower lovers will delight in this double dose of the delicious crucifer. Pureed cauliflower combines with curry powder, broth, and coconut milk for a seductively creamy soup that is accented with crisp-roasted bits of cauliflower "rice."

1 large cauliflower, center core and leaves removed
1½ tablespoons olive oil
1 yellow onion, finely minced
2 tablespoons curry powder, hot or mild
3 cups vegetable broth

Salt and freshly ground black pepper
1 (13-ounce) can unsweetened coconut milk, or 1½ cups unsweetened nondairy milk
Minced fresh parsley or cilantro, for garnish
Lemon wedges, to serve (optional)

Preheat the oven to 425°F. Oil a baking sheet and set aside. Using a box grater with large holes, grate enough of the raw cauliflower florets to equal 2 cups. Set aside.

Cut the remaining cauliflower into small pieces. Heat 1 tablespoon of the oil in a large pot over medium heat. Add the onion and cauliflower pieces, cover, and cook until softened, 5 minutes. Sprinkle on the curry powder, stirring until fragrant, 1 minute. Add the broth and bring to a boil. Reduce the heat to medium and season to taste with salt and pepper. Simmer until the vegetables are tender, about 8 minutes.

While the soup is simmering, toss the grated cauliflower with the remaining ½ tablespoon oil and spread evenly on the prepared baking sheet. Season to taste with salt and pepper. Roast, stirring occasionally, until tender and golden brown, about 10 minutes. Set aside.

When the soup is done simmering, remove the pot from the heat and puree with an immersion blender. Or transfer to a stand blender or food processor and puree in batches, then return to the pot. Stir in the coconut milk and heat until hot. Taste and adjust the seasonings. To serve, ladle into bowls and top with the roasted cauliflower "rice" and parsley. Accompany with lemon wedges if desired.

last-minute laksa

serves 4

If you enjoy the fragrant flavors of Southeast Asia, you'll love laksa. A brothy blend of seasonings, including a healthy dose of heat, provides the backdrop for creamy diced tofu and chewy noodles. A garnish of fresh bean sprouts and cilantro contribute a refreshing accent.

2 large shallots, halved
1 tablespoon Asian chili paste
2 teaspoons grated fresh ginger
2 teaspoons ground coriander
1 teaspoon curry powder
4 cups vegetable broth
1 tablespoon neutral vegetable oil
8 ounces extra-firm tofu, cut into
   ½-inch dice
4 scallions, minced
½ cup frozen green peas, partially thawed

1 teaspoon soy sauce
1½ teaspoons sugar
1 teaspoon salt
¼ teaspoon freshly ground black pepper
1 (13-ounce) can unsweetened coconut milk
2 tablespoons freshly squeezed lime juice
3 cups cooked linguine or rice noodles
   (8 ounces uncooked)
1 cup fresh bean sprouts
¼ cup coarsely chopped fresh cilantro

In a food processor, combine the shallots, chili paste, ginger, coriander, curry powder, and ¼ cup of the broth, and process to a paste.

Heat the oil in a large pot over medium heat. Add the seasoning paste mixture and cook, stirring, until fragrant, 2 minutes. Do not burn. Stir in the remaining 3¾ cups broth and bring to a boil. Reduce the heat to medium, add the tofu, scallions, peas, soy sauce, sugar, 1 teaspoon salt or to taste, and the pepper, and simmer until hot, 10 minutes.

Add the coconut milk, lime juice, and noodles, and simmer to heat through and blend the flavors, 5 minutes. Taste and adjust the seasonings. To serve, ladle the soup into bowls and garnish with bean sprouts and cilantro.

moroccan-spiced pumpkin soup

serves 4

The exotic spices of Morocco transform canned pumpkin into a sensational soup that is ready in minutes. For more heat, add more cayenne or include a minced chile when you add the ginger. For added creaminess, add a spoonful of vegan sour cream to each bowl when serving.

1 tablespoon olive oil
1 yellow onion, finely chopped
1½ teaspoons grated fresh ginger
1 teaspoon ground coriander
1 teaspoon ground cinnamon
1 teaspoon light brown sugar
¼ teaspoon ground allspice
1 teaspoon salt

¼ teaspoon freshly ground black pepper
⅛ teaspoon cayenne
2 teaspoons agave nectar
1 (15-ounce) can pumpkin puree
2½ cups vegetable broth
1½ cups nondairy milk
¼ cup coarsely chopped pistachios

Heat the oil in a large pot over medium heat. Add the onion, cover, and cook until softened, 5 minutes. Stir in the ginger, coriander, cinnamon, brown sugar, allspice, 1 teaspoon salt or to taste, the pepper, cayenne, and agave, then add the pumpkin and slowly add the broth, stirring to blend until smooth. Simmer until the onion is tender and the flavors are well combined, 10 minutes. Stir in the nondairy milk and cook until hot, 5 minutes longer. Serve hot garnished with the pistachios.

miso soup with tofu and dulse

serves 4

Although miso soup is often enjoyed without embellishment, I like to add tofu to make it more substantial, and ginger and other seasonings for extra flavor. Dulse is a dried sea vegetable available at natural food stores. It makes a tasty and nutrient-rich addition to this soup, although it can be omitted if unavailable.

2 teaspoons neutral vegetable oil
2 teaspoons minced fresh ginger
4 scallions, minced
5 cups vegetable broth
⅓ cup light miso paste

8 ounces firm tofu, cut into ½-inch dice
½ cup torn dulse
1 tablespoon mirin
2 to 3 teaspoons soy sauce

Heat the oil in a large pot over medium heat. Add the ginger and scallions, and cook until fragrant, about 1 minute. Add the broth and bring to a boil. Reduce the heat to medium and simmer to blend flavors, 10 minutes. Remove about 1 cup of broth and blend it in a bowl with the miso paste until smooth. Stir the miso mixture back into the pot. Be careful not to boil. Add the tofu, dulse, mirin, and as much soy sauce as needed, depending on the saltiness of your broth. Taste and adjust the seasonings. Serve hot.

note: Be sure to carefully inspect the dulse leaves before using to remove any tiny hard bits that may be in the folds of the leaves.

asian noodle soup with bok choy and shiitakes

serves 4

The hint of heat from the sriracha and ginger make this soup a good choice to ward off winter chills. I love the way the rice noodles play off the vegetables, and the fragrant accent of cilantro or Thai basil brings it all together. Tender baby bok choy is wonderful in this soup—use about 3 heads of small baby bok choy to substitute for one regular size bok choy.

6 ounces thin rice noodles
1 tablespoon neutral vegetable oil
3 cloves garlic, minced
5 scallions, minced
1 small carrot, grated
2 teaspoons grated fresh ginger
1 bok choy, finely sliced
  (about 4 cups)

1½ cups thinly sliced shiitake mushroom
  caps
5 cups vegetable broth
¼ cup soy sauce
1 teaspoon sriracha sauce
Salt and freshly ground black pepper
½ cup chopped fresh cilantro or Thai basil
  leaves

Cook the noodles in a pot of boiling salted water until just tender, 3 to 4 minutes. Drain and rinse in cold water to stop the cooking process. Set aside. Heat the oil in a large pot over medium heat. Add the garlic, scallions, carrot, ginger, bok choy, and mushrooms. Cook, stirring, until softened, about 2 minutes. Stir in the broth, soy sauce, 1 teaspoon sriracha or to taste, and salt and pepper to taste. Bring to a boil, then reduce the heat to a simmer and cook until the vegetables are tender, about 5 minutes. Stir in the reserved noodles. Taste and adjust the seasonings. To serve, ladle into bowls and top with the cilantro.

chard and red lentil soup

serves 4 to 6

When you want lentils in a hurry, red lentils are the ones to choose. Unlike other varieties that can take up to an hour to cook, red lentils are tender in about 15 minutes, making them an ideal quick-fix ingredient. Paired with chard here (although spinach may be substituted), the lentils make for a colorful soup that is satisfying and delicious.

1 tablespoon olive oil
1 yellow onion, shredded
2 carrots, shredded
3 cloves garlic, minced
1 teaspoon ground cumin
½ teaspoon ground coriander
¼ teaspoon cayenne

1 (14.5-ounce) can diced tomatoes,
   including juice
¾ cup dried red lentils
4 cups vegetable broth
Salt
¼ teaspoon freshly ground black pepper
4 cups coarsely chopped chard (8 ounces)

Heat the oil in a large pot over medium heat. Add the onion, carrots, and garlic. Cover and cook until softened, 5 minutes. Stir in the cumin, coriander, and ¼ teaspoon cayenne or to taste, then add the tomatoes, lentils, broth, ½ teaspoon salt or to taste, and the pepper. Bring to a boil, then reduce the heat to medium and simmer, partially covered, until the lentils are tender, about 15 minutes. About 4 minutes before it is ready to serve, add the chard, stirring to wilt. Taste and adjust the seasonings. Serve hot.

speedy sandwiches

A sandwich may be the ultimate quick-fix meal, and the ones in this chapter are no exception. What is exceptional about these recipes is how fabulous they taste, while at the same time, they are satisfying and nutritious. The Vietnamese Tofu Wraps, inspired by the classic báhn mì sandwich, combine a symphony of flavors and textures in one delicious sandwich. Same goes for the luscious Niçoise Salad Wraps, bursting with olive tapenade and fresh basil, and the creamy-crunchy Indonesian Satay Sandwiches with Peanut Sauce. If a burger is more your style, there are Black Bean Sunburgers and some amazing "Freeburgers," so named because they're gluten- and soy-free. Serve on toasted buns topped with the works and chips, a pickle, and maybe some slaw on the side.

Other favorites include Sloppy portobellos, Seitan Gyros served with a refreshing tzatziki sauce, and two kinds of burritos—zesty Black Bean and Green Salsa Burritos and the Burrito Scramble, ideal for a satisfying breakfast or lunch.

chesapeake chickpea sandwiches

serves 4

This is a vegan version of my crab cake recipe from my days as a chef in a seafood restaurant. Chickpeas seasoned with sea vegetable flakes replace the crab.

1½ cups home-cooked chickpeas,
   or 1 (15-ounce) can, drained and rinsed
3 tablespoons panko crumbs
2 tablespoons chickpea flour
3 scallions, minced
2 tablespoons minced fresh parsley
2 tablespoons vegan mayonnaise, plus
   more for spreading
1 tablespoon freshly squeezed lemon juice
1 teaspoon spicy brown mustard
1 teaspoon nori, dulse, or other sea
   vegetable flakes (see note)

1 teaspoon finely minced capers
½ teaspoon vegan Worcestershire sauce
½ teaspoon Old Bay Seasoning
½ teaspoon salt
¼ teaspoon freshly ground black pepper
⅛ teaspoon cayenne
1 tablespoon olive oil
4 sandwich rolls, split and toasted
4 lettuce leaves
4 slices ripe tomato
Hot sauce

In a food processor, process the chickpeas until broken up. Add the panko, flour, scallions, parsley, the 2 tablespoons mayonnaise, the lemon juice, mustard, nori flakes, capers, Worcestershire sauce, Old Bay Seasoning, salt, pepper, and cayenne and pulse until well mixed with some texture remaining. Scoop out the mixture and divide into 4 equal portions. Use your hands to press each portion into a patty (about the same diameter as your rolls). Set aside.

Heat the oil in a large nonstick skillet over medium heat. Add the chickpea cakes and cook until nicely browned on the bottom, about 5 minutes. Carefully turn the cakes and cook on the other side until browned.

To assemble, spread vegan mayonnaise on each of the rolls and layer each with lettuce, tomato, and a chickpea cake. Serve immediately with hot sauce on the side.

note: You can find small shakers of nutrient-rich nori, dulse, and other dried sea vegetables in natural food stores.

barbecue pinto–portobello sandwiches

serves 4

Mushrooms and pintos soak up the flavor of zesty barbecue sauce in this hearty sandwich. Serve with creamy coleslaw for a delectable lunch. I use the shredding disc on my food processor to quickly and easily shred the mushrooms. For a smokier flavor, substitute 2 minced chipotle chiles in adobo for the chopped green chiles.

1 tablespoon olive oil
½ cup minced onion
3 cloves garlic, minced
2 large portobello mushrooms, shredded or thinly sliced
1½ cups home-cooked pinto beans, or 1 (15-ounce) can, drained and rinsed
1 cup tomato puree
¼ cup canned chopped green chiles, hot or mild

1 tablespoon yellow mustard
1 tablespoon molasses
1 tablespoon agave nectar or maple syrup
2 teaspoons chili powder
1 teaspoon Liquid Smoke
½ teaspoon smoked paprika
Salt and freshly ground black pepper
4 sandwich rolls, split and toasted

Heat the oil in a saucepan over medium heat. Add the onion and garlic and cook until softened, 5 minutes. Stir in the mushrooms and cook until softened, 3 minutes. Stir in the pinto beans, tomato puree, chiles, mustard, molasses, agave, chili powder, Liquid Smoke, smoked paprika, and salt and pepper to taste. Cook, stirring occasionally, to heat through and blend the flavors, about 7 minutes. To serve, spoon onto rolls.

black bean and green salsa burritos

serves 4

Try these for a change of pace from the usual red bean burrito. In these wholesome and satisfying burritos, black beans share the spotlight with four flavors of green: chiles, salsa verde, cilantro, and avocado. You can use store-bought salsa verde, or make Tomatillo–Cilantro Salsa (see page 175). For extra flavor and texture, add any or all of the following to your burritos before rolling them up: chopped ripe tomato, vegan sour cream, sliced black olives, or minced scallions.

1 ripe avocado
1 tablespoon olive oil
1 small yellow onion, minced
2 cloves garlic, minced
¼ cup canned chopped green chiles,
   hot or mild
1½ cups home-cooked black beans, or
   1 (15-ounce) can, drained and rinsed

2 teaspoons chili powder
1 cup green salsa (salsa verde), store-
   bought or homemade
3 tablespoons chopped fresh cilantro
Salt and freshly ground black pepper
4 (10-inch) flour tortillas, warmed
Chopped tomato

Halve and pit the avocado, spoon out the flesh, and cut into thin strips. Set aside. Heat the oil in a saucepan over medium heat. Add the onion and garlic and cook until softened, 5 minutes. Add the chiles, beans, chili powder, and ½ cup of the salsa, stirring to combine and heat through. Use the back of a fork to mash some of the beans as they cook. Stir in the cilantro and season to taste with salt and pepper.

To serve, spoon one-quarter of the mixture down the center of a tortilla, top with a few strips of the reserved avocado, chopped tomato, and a spoonful of the remaining salsa. Roll up into a burrito, tucking in the sides as you roll. Repeat with the remaining ingredients. Serve immediately.

seitan and slaw wraps

serves 4

These fabulous wraps have it all: chewy seitan coated in a luscious spicy-sweet glaze all wrapped up with a zesty Asian-inspired slaw. Instead of serving as wraps, you can serve the seitan and slaw on toasted rolls or skip the bread altogether and serve as a salad with the seitan arranged on top of the slaw.

2 teaspoons neutral vegetable oil
½ red onion, thinly sliced
8 ounces seitan, cut into ¼-inch strips
3 tablespoons sweet Thai chili sauce
2 teaspoons sriracha sauce, or more
 if needed
Salt and freshly ground black pepper

3 cups finely shredded cabbage
½ cup fresh cilantro leaves
2 tablespoons rice vinegar
2 teaspoons agave nectar or sugar
Vegan mayonnaise
4 (10-inch) flour tortillas

Heat the oil in a skillet over medium heat. Add the onion and cook until softened, 4 minutes. Add the seitan and cook, stirring, until browned, 5 to 7 minutes. Add the Thai chili sauce, 1 teaspoon of the sriracha, and salt and pepper to taste. Cook, stirring, to coat and blend the flavors, 2 minutes. Remove from the heat and set aside.

In a bowl, combine the cabbage, cilantro, rice vinegar, agave, the remaining 1 teaspoon sriracha, and salt and pepper to taste. Toss to mix well.

To serve, spread vegan mayonnaise on a tortilla, dotting with extra sriracha, if desired. Spoon a line of the seitan mixture down the center of the tortilla. Top with a portion of the slaw, then roll up into a wrap. Repeat with the remaining ingredients.

freeburgers

serves 4

These tasty burgers are completely free: soy- and gluten-free, that is. Because they're baked, they're also relatively low in fat. And they're versatile, too—use any kind of cooked beans that you like; black beans or chickpeas are good choices. You can serve them on burger rolls with all the trimmings, in a wrap sandwich, or on a plate, topped with a sauce.

1½ cups home-cooked dark red kidney beans, or 1 (15-ounce) can, mashed
¼ cup chopped scallions
⅓ cup finely ground walnuts
2 tablespoons brown rice flour
2 tablespoons chickpea flour, plus more for coating burgers
1 tablespoon tapioca flour
1 tablespoon olive oil

2 tablespoons vegetable broth
½ teaspoon garlic powder
½ teaspoon onion powder
½ teaspoon paprika
¼ teaspoon salt
⅛ teaspoon freshly ground black pepper
4 toasted burger rolls
Condiments of choice

Preheat the oven to 400°F. Generously oil a baking sheet and set aside. In a food processor, combine the beans, scallions, walnuts, brown rice flour, the 2 tablespoons chickpea flour, and the tapioca flour. Add the oil, broth, garlic powder, onion powder, paprika, salt, and pepper and process until well blended.

Dust your hands with a little chickpea flour (the mixture will be sticky). Divide the mixture into 4 equal pieces and shape into thin patties. Arrange on the prepared baking sheet. Bake the patties until golden brown, turning once, 8 to 10 minutes per side. Serve hot on burger rolls, topped with your favorite condiments.

curried chickpea patties in pitas

serves 4

Crisply fried patties seasoned with curry combine with creamy chutney mayonnaise and shredded lettuce for a wonderful flavor combination. The recipe calls for pitas because they're readily available, but if you can find Indian flatbreads, such as roti, use them instead.

1½ tablespoons olive oil
½ cup chopped onion
2 cloves garlic, minced
2 tablespoons curry powder, hot or mild
½ teaspoon ground coriander
½ teaspoon ground cumin
1½ cups home-cooked chickpeas, or
   1 (15-ounce) can, drained and rinsed

2 tablespoons chickpea flour
1 tablespoon water
Salt and freshly ground black pepper
½ cup mango chutney
⅓ cup vegan mayonnaise
4 (7-inch) pita pockets
Shredded lettuce

Heat ½ tablespoon of the oil in a skillet over medium heat. Add the onion and garlic, cover, and cook until softened, 4 minutes. Add the curry powder, coriander, and cumin, stirring to coat. Transfer the onion mixture to a food processor, add the chickpeas, chickpea flour, water, and salt and pepper to taste. Process to mix well. Taste and adjust the seasonings. Shape the mixture into 4 large or 8 small patties and set aside.

Heat the remaining 1 tablespoon oil in a large skillet over medium heat. Add the patties and cook until browned on both sides, turning once, about 5 minutes per side.

Finely chop any large pieces of mango in the chutney. In a small bowl, combine the chutney and mayonnaise and mix well to combine. Spread the chutney mixture inside each of the pita pockets and stuff some lettuce into each pocket followed by 1 or 2 chickpea patties, depending on the size. Serve hot.

black bean sunburgers

serves 4

Burgers are often the answer when you need a quick and easy meal. But why settle for expensive packaged burgers when it's so easy (and economical) to make your own? Made with black beans, sunflower seeds, and vital wheat gluten flour, these delicious and sturdy burgers are ready in minutes. They also freeze well, so make an extra batch to have on hand.

½ cup sunflower seeds
¼ cup chopped onion
1½ cups home-cooked black beans, or
   1 (15-ounce) can, drained and rinsed
⅓ cup vital wheat gluten flour, or more
   if needed

2 tablespoons soy sauce
½ teaspoon smoked paprika
Salt and freshly ground black pepper
Olive oil, for frying
4 toasted burger rolls
Condiments of choice

In a food processor, pulse the sunflower seeds until coarsely ground. Add the onion, black beans, vital wheat gluten flour, soy sauce, paprika, and salt and pepper to taste. Process until well combined, but with some texture remaining.

Shape the mixture into 4 patties, adding a little more wheat gluten flour if the mixture is too wet.

Heat a thin layer of oil in a large skillet over medium heat. Add the burgers and cook until browned on both sides, turning once, about 4 minutes per side. Serve hot on burger rolls, topped with your favorite condiments.

vietnamese tofu wraps

serves 4

These flavorful wraps have all the bold flavors and textures of bánh mì sandwiches, but without the French bread. At first I wondered if I'd miss the baguette, but after my first bite there was no doubt—these wraps are absolutely sublime.

1 tablespoon neutral vegetable oil

1 pound extra-firm tofu, drained and cut into ¼-inch strips

3 tablespoons hoisin sauce

2 tablespoons soy sauce

1 teaspoon sriracha sauce, plus more for serving

4 (10-inch) flour tortillas or other flatbread

Vegan mayonnaise

1 cucumber, seeded and thinly sliced

1 carrot, shredded

1 cup fresh cilantro leaves

2 tablespoons chopped bottled jalapeños

Heat the oil in a skillet over medium heat. Add the tofu and cook until golden brown, turning frequently, 7 to 10 minutes. Add the hoisin, soy sauce, and the 1 teaspoon sriracha, stirring gently to coat the tofu. Remove from the heat and set aside to cool.

To assemble the wraps, spread the tortillas with the vegan mayonnaise and drizzle with sriracha to taste. Arrange one-quarter of the tofu strips down the center of each of the tortillas. Top with cucumber, carrot, cilantro, and jalapeños. Roll up each wrap tightly and serve at once.

mediterranean quesadillas

serves 4

A who's who of vibrant Mediterranean flavors merges deliciously in these tasty sandwiches inspired by quesadillas. Creamy mashed white beans provide the base for the filling that is studded with bits of olives, sun-dried tomatoes, artichoke hearts, and roasted red bell pepper. If your white beans are a little dry when mashing them, add 2 to 3 teaspoons of olive oil, water, or lemon juice to make them creamier.

1 tablespoon olive oil
½ cup chopped red onion
3 cloves garlic, minced
½ cup chopped roasted red bell pepper
   (see page 16)
1 cup canned artichoke hearts, chopped
1½ cups home-cooked white beans, or
   1 (15-ounce) can, drained and mashed

¼ cup pitted kalamata olives, chopped
2 tablespoons oil-packed sun-dried
   tomatoes
Salt and freshly ground black pepper
4 (10-inch) flour tortillas
½ cup fresh basil leaves

Heat the oil in a skillet over medium heat. Add the onion and garlic and cook until softened, 5 minutes. Add the roasted red bell pepper, artichoke hearts, beans, olives, and sun-dried tomatoes. Stir to mix well. Season to taste with salt and pepper.

Arrange the tortillas on a flat work surface. Divide the bean and vegetable mixture among the tortillas and spread evenly. Top each with the basil and fold the tortillas over, pressing down to hold them together.

Heat a large nonstick skillet over medium heat. Add one or two of the quesadillas (depending on the size of your pan) and cook until nicely browned on one side, 1 to 2 minutes. Carefully flip over and brown the other side. Keep the quesadillas warm while you cook the rest. Serve hot.

burrito scramble

serves 4

I adore a good tofu scramble, and I'm an ardent fan of burritos, too. It should be no surprise, then, that I combined these two favorites into one satisfying dish. Delicious any time of day, these bountiful burritos are filled with a zesty tofu scramble made with green chiles, red onion, and salsa.

1 ripe Hass avocado (optional)
1 tablespoon olive oil
½ cup minced red onion
3 cloves garlic, minced
1 (4-ounce) can chopped green chiles, hot
  or mild
1 pound extra-firm tofu, drained and
  crumbled

3 tablespoons nutritional yeast
1 teaspoon chili powder
½ teaspoon ground cumin
Salt and freshly ground black pepper
4 (10-inch) flour tortillas
1 cup tomato salsa, hot or mild
½ cup fresh cilantro leaves

Halve and pit the avocado, if using, spoon out the flesh, and cut into thin slices. Set aside. Heat the oil in a skillet over medium heat. Add the onion and garlic and cook until softened, 5 minutes. Add the chiles, tofu, nutritional yeast, chili powder, cumin, and salt and pepper to taste. Cook, stirring, to heat through and mix well, about 7 minutes. To assemble, arrange the tortillas on a flat work surface. Spoon the tofu mixture down the center of each tortilla. Top with salsa, cilantro, and the reserved avocado. Roll up the burritos and serve immediately.

sloppy portobellos

serves 4

Sloppy Joes are one of my favorite sandwiches, and over the years I've made countless variations using everything from tempeh and seitan to beans and bulgur. This time, the vehicle for all the delicious sloppiness is shredded portobello mushrooms, and I think it may be my favorite version so far.

1 tablespoon olive oil
½ cup minced onion
2 cloves garlic, minced
12 ounces portobello mushrooms, shredded
    or finely chopped
1 (4-ounce) can chopped green chiles,
    drained
1 tablespoon soy sauce

⅔ cup ketchup
2 teaspoons prepared yellow mustard
1 tablespoon chili powder
½ teaspoon Liquid Smoke
½ teaspoon salt
¼ teaspoon freshly ground black pepper
4 toasted burger rolls

In a large saucepan, heat the oil over medium heat. Add the onion, cover, and cook until softened, 4 minutes. Add the garlic and cook until fragrant, 30 seconds. Stir in the mushrooms, chiles, and soy sauce and cook until lightly browned, 2 to 3 minutes.

Stir in the ketchup, mustard, chili powder, Liquid Smoke, salt, and pepper. Mix well, adding a little water if the mixture is too dry. Simmer to blend the flavors, 5 minutes.

When ready to serve, spoon the mixture onto the rolls and serve hot.

seitan gyros with tzatziki sauce

serves 4

These gyros gone vegan are made with thinly sliced seitan. Seasoned with rosemary, oregano, and lemon juice, the chewy seitan is topped with a cooling tzatziki sauce, shredded lettuce, and chopped tomato, all wrapped up in a warm flatbread. What's the Greek word for "yum"?

TZATZIKI SAUCE
½ small cucumber, seeded and quartered
2 cloves garlic, chopped
½ cup vegan yogurt
1 tablespoon freshly squeezed lemon juice
2 tablespoons chopped fresh dill, mint, or parsley
Salt and freshly ground black pepper

1 tablespoon olive oil
8 ounces seitan, thinly sliced
1 teaspoon dried oregano
1 teaspoon dried rosemary
½ teaspoon salt
¼ teaspoon freshly ground black pepper
2 tablespoons red wine vinegar
2 tablespoons freshly squeezed lemon juice
4 pitas or other flatbreads, warmed
1 large ripe tomato, chopped
1 cup shredded lettuce
½ cup chopped red onion (optional)

To make the tzatziki, in a food processor, combine the cucumber, garlic, yogurt, lemon juice, dill, and salt and pepper to taste. Process until well blended, then transfer to a bowl. Taste and adjust the seasoning and set aside.

Heat the oil in a skillet over medium heat. Add the seitan and cook until browned, about 5 minutes. Add the oregano and rosemary, and season to taste with salt and pepper. Add the vinegar and lemon juice, tossing to coat.

To assemble, divide the seitan mixture among the pita loaves, top with the reserved sauce, and sprinkle with tomato, lettuce, and onion if desired. Serve immediately.

indonesian satay sandwiches with peanut sauce

serves 4

The rich and creamy peanut sauce envelops chewy seitan and crunchy shredded cabbage and carrot in this outstanding sandwich. Use soft Middle Eastern or Indian flatbreads for these, if you can find them. If you're not a fan of cabbage, shredded lettuce may be substituted.

1 clove garlic, finely minced
½ cup creamy peanut butter
2 tablespoons hoisin sauce
1 tablespoon rice vinegar
2 teaspoons light brown sugar
1 teaspoon sriracha sauce
½ cup vegetable broth

1 tablespoon neutral vegetable oil
12 ounces seitan, cut into ¼-inch strips
Salt and freshly ground black pepper
4 (10-inch) lavash, flour tortillas, or pitas
1½ cups finely shredded cabbage
1 carrot, shredded
1 ripe tomato, chopped

In a bowl, combine the garlic, peanut butter, hoisin, rice vinegar, sugar, and sriracha and mix well. Slowly stir in the broth to make a smooth sauce. Taste and adjust the seasonings and set aside.

Heat the oil in a skillet over medium heat. Add the seitan and season to taste with salt and pepper. Cook until browned all over, 6 to 8 minutes. Add the reserved peanut sauce and toss to coat.

To serve, divide the seitan among the flatbreads. Top with cabbage, carrot, and tomato. Roll up and serve immediately.

avocado, dulse, lettuce, and tomato sandwiches

serves 4

In case you're wondering about putting sea vegetables on a sandwich, hear me out. Dulse is different from other sea vegetables. Its soft dried leaves are reddish purple, not green or black, and when the leaves are fried in oil, they become crisp like bacon with a faint salty-smoky flavor. Plus, sea vegetables are among the most nutrient-rich ingredients on the planet, and this is a fun way to enjoy them. Dulse is available at natural food stores. For this recipe, you need the whole dulse leaves, not flakes or powder. Be sure to clean the leaves carefully before using as some hard particles may be hidden in the folds of the leaves. (If you're still not convinced, you can make these sandwiches with tempeh bacon instead.)

1 or 2 ripe Hass avocados
1 tablespoon olive oil
1 cup dulse (see headnote)
Vegan mayonnaise, for spreading

8 slices bread of choice, lightly toasted
Lettuce leaves (enough for 4 sandwiches)
1 to 2 ripe tomatoes, sliced
Salt and freshly ground black pepper

Halve and pit the avocado, spoon out the flesh, and cut into thin slices. Set aside. Heat the oil in a skillet over medium heat. Add the dulse and cook until lightly crisped, turning once, 1 to 2 minutes per side. (Dulse can burn easily, so watch it carefully.) Spread the mayonnaise on the bread slices and top four of them with lettuce, tomato slices, and a few pieces of the dulse. Top with slices of the reserved avocado and season to taste with salt and pepper. Top each sandwich with a remaining slice of bread. Cut the sandwiches in half and serve immediately.

niçoise salad wraps

serves 4

These wraps were inspired by my love of both niçoise salad and the famous muffuletta sandwich of New Orleans that features a tangy olive spread. Light yet satisfying, niçoise salad wraps are perfect for those days when you want a tasty salad but are in the mood for a sandwich. Colorful and loaded with flavor, these yummy wraps let you have your salad—and sandwich, too!

2 tablespoons olive oil
12 ounces extra-firm tofu, thinly sliced
1 teaspoon soy sauce
1½ tablespoons balsamic vinegar
Salt and freshly ground black pepper
3 cups shredded lettuce
½ teaspoon sugar
4 (10-inch) flour tortillas or other
  flatbreads

Vegan mayonnaise, for spreading
⅓ to ½ cup black or green olive tapenade
  (see note)
1 roasted red bell pepper, jarred or
  homemade (see page 16), cut into strips
1 ripe tomato, thinly sliced
½ cup fresh basil leaves

Heat 1 tablespoon of oil in a large skillet over medium heat. Add the tofu and cook until lightly browned and slightly crisped, about 8 minutes. Sprinkle on the soy sauce, ½ tablespoon of the vinegar, and salt and pepper to taste. Remove from the heat and set aside. Place the lettuce in a bowl. Add the remaining 1 tablespoon oil, the remaining 1 tablespoon vinegar, the sugar, and salt and pepper to taste. Toss to combine.

To assemble, spread the tortillas with the vegan mayonnaise followed by the tapenade. Arrange the tofu slices down the center of each tortilla and top with the bell pepper, tomato, basil, and the reserved lettuce. Roll up and serve immediately.

note: If tapenade is unavailable, combine in a food processor: ½ cup pitted black or green olives, 2 teaspoons capers, a small crushed garlic clove, and a splash of lemon juice and process to a paste.

chapter 7

snappy
salads

We all know it's important to eat more fresh vegetables and what better way to enjoy them than in a salad? Rather than just a few lettuce leaves tossed in a bowl as an afterthought, I prefer to make the salad a star of the show and as flavorful and texturally interesting as any other type of dish. Most of the salads in this chapter can be enjoyed as a main dish and make a satisfying lunch in themselves. Others are ideal side dishes to complement a meal.

There are hearty noodle salads such as Soba Slaw, Rainbow Rotini Salad, and Sicilian-Style Orzo Salad with Walnuts and Raisins. Grain-centric salads such as Curried Rice and Chickpea Salad, and Quinoa Salad with Apples and Walnuts, are nutritional powerhouses that taste as good as they look. Among the delicious main dish salads are the colorful Black Bean and Sweet Potato Salad and my personal favorite, the Deconstructed Báhn Mì Salad, served with slices of toasted baguette, spread lightly with a spicy vegan mayonnaise.

black bean and sweet potato salad

serves 4

The dramatic color combination of sweet potatoes and black beans is outshone only by the fantastic flavors in this salad. With its nutty crunch of pecans and luscious lime and cumin dressing, this salad makes a great main dish lunch.

2 sweet potatoes, peeled and diced
1½ cups home-cooked black beans, or
   1 (15-ounce) can, drained and rinsed
½ cup chopped yellow bell pepper
⅓ cup chopped toasted pecans
¼ cup minced red onion
¼ cup minced celery
¼ cup chopped fresh cilantro or parsley
1 hot chile, seeded and minced (optional)

2 tablespoons olive oil
2 tablespoons freshly squeezed lime juice
2 teaspoons agave nectar, or 1 teaspoon
   sugar
½ teaspoon salt
¼ teaspoon ground cumin
¼ teaspoon ground coriander
¼ teaspoon freshly ground black pepper

Steam the sweet potatoes over boiling water until just tender, about 15 minutes. While the potatoes are cooking, in a large bowl, combine the beans, bell pepper, pecans, onion, celery, cilantro, and chile, if using, and set aside.

In a small bowl, combine the oil, lime juice, agave, salt, cumin, coriander, and pepper. Pour the dressing over the salad. Add the sweet potatoes and toss gently to combine. Taste and adjust the seasonings. Serve at once, or cover and refrigerate until needed.

panzanella with grilled vegetables

serves 4

Grilling the vegetables transforms an otherwise everyday panzanella (a classic Italian bread salad) into one extraordinary experience. For a heartier salad that can be enjoyed as a main dish, add some cooked chickpeas.

1 clove garlic, minced
2 tablespoons red wine vinegar
1 teaspoon sugar
½ teaspoon salt
¼ teaspoon freshly ground black pepper
4 tablespoons olive oil
½ pound day-old crusty Italian bread, thickly sliced

1 large red bell pepper, halved lengthwise
1 large red onion, thickly sliced
1 cup white mushrooms
3 large ripe tomatoes, thickly sliced
½ cup pitted kalamata olives, halved
2 teaspoons capers
¼ cup chopped fresh Italian parsley
¼ cup torn fresh basil leaves

In a small bowl, combine the garlic, vinegar, sugar, salt, and pepper. Whisk in the olive oil and blend until smooth. Set aside.

Lightly oil the grill and preheat until hot. Place the bread slices on the grill and grill until golden brown on both sides, turning once. Remove and set aside to cool. Arrange the bell pepper, onion, and mushrooms on the grill and grill the vegetables until slightly tender, turning once, about 10 minutes. Remove the vegetables from the grill and set aside. Arrange the tomato slices on the grill and grill until light grill marks appear, 2 minutes per side. Remove from the grill and set aside.

Cut the reserved bread and vegetables into bite-size pieces and combine in a large bowl. Add the olives, capers, parsley, and basil. Pour the reserved dressing onto the salad and toss to combine. Serve immediately.

burmese ginger salad

serves 4

This unusual salad is a spin-off of a hauntingly delicious Burmese salad made with hard-to-find fermented tea leaves. This version uses readily available pickled ginger but retains its exotic pedigree. Crispy fried garlic is available in Asian markets.

2 teaspoons toasted sesame oil
1 teaspoon finely minced hot chile
2 teaspoons soy sauce
½ cup finely chopped pickled ginger
   (see note)
1 tablespoon peanut oil
4 cloves garlic, cut into slivers, or
   1 tablespoon crispy fried garlic

3½ cups finely shredded romaine lettuce
½ cup roasted peanuts, slightly crushed
⅓ cup sunflower seeds
1 tablespoon toasted sesame seeds
1 large ripe tomato, finely chopped
2 tablespoons freshly squeezed lemon or
   lime juice
Lemon or lime wedges, for garnish

Heat the sesame oil in a small pan over medium heat. Add the chile and cook, stirring occasionally, until slightly softened, 1 minute. Remove from the heat, and stir in the soy sauce and pickled ginger. Set aside.

Unless using crispy fried garlic, heat the peanut oil in a small skillet over medium heat. Add the garlic and cook, stirring, until golden brown. (Be careful not to burn.) Remove the garlic with a slotted spoon and set aside on paper towels.

Spread the lettuce on a large platter. Spoon the ginger mixture into the center of the lettuce, then surround with separate mounds of the peanuts, sunflower seeds, sesame seeds, tomato, and fried garlic. Drizzle with the lemon juice. Serve at once garnished with lemon wedges. Or, the salad ingredients may be combined in a bowl and tossed before serving.

note: Instead of pickled ginger, you may use fresh young ginger that should be sautéed along with the chile (instead of adding it afterward, as for the pickled ginger).

moroccan-spiced couscous tabbouleh

serves 4

This salad couldn't be faster or more flavorful thanks to quick-cooking couscous and an array of Moroccan seasonings. Fresh vegetables and herbs provide the refreshing texture that tabbouleh is noted for, and the chickpeas offer added protein.

1 cup couscous

1 ripe tomato, chopped

¼ cup minced red onion

½ English cucumber, seeded and chopped

1½ cups home-cooked chickpeas, or
   1 (15-ounce) can, drained and rinsed

¼ cup chopped fresh mint leaves

¼ cup chopped fresh parsley

1 teaspoon ground coriander

1 teaspoon ground ginger

½ teaspoon ground cumin

½ teaspoon ground turmeric

¼ teaspoon ground allspice or cinnamon

¼ teaspoon sugar

⅛ teaspoon cayenne

½ teaspoon salt

2 tablespoons freshly squeezed lemon juice

3 tablespoons olive oil

Bring 1 cup of salted water to a boil in a saucepan. Add the couscous, cover, and remove from the heat. Set aside for 10 minutes. Meanwhile, in a large bowl, combine the tomato, onion, cucumber, chickpeas, mint, and parsley. Set aside.

In a small bowl, combine the coriander, ginger, cumin, turmeric, allspice, sugar, cayenne, and salt. Add the lemon juice and olive oil and mix well. Add the reserved couscous to the vegetables and pour on the dressing. Toss gently to combine. Serve at once, or cover and refrigerate until needed.

soba slaw

serves 4

Chewy soba noodles provide the backdrop for this satisfying slaw, bursting with color, texture, and flavor. If you prefer a spicy slaw, add a teaspoon or so of sriracha sauce to give it some heat.

8 ounces soba noodles
3 cups finely shredded cabbage
1 cup grated carrot
3 scallions, minced
2 tablespoons chopped fresh cilantro or
    parsley
2 teaspoons grated fresh ginger

3 tablespoons rice vinegar
1½ tablespoons neutral vegetable oil
1½ tablespoons soy sauce
2 teaspoons toasted sesame oil
½ teaspoon sugar
Salt
2 tablespoons chopped peanuts

Cook the noodles in a pot of boiling salted water until tender. Drain and run under cold water, then transfer to a large bowl. Add the cabbage, carrot, scallions, cilantro, and ginger. Set aside.

In a small bowl, combine the vinegar, vegetable oil, soy sauce, sesame oil, sugar, and salt to taste. Stir until well blended.

Pour the dressing over the noodles and vegetables and toss gently to coat. Taste and adjust the seasoning. Sprinkle the peanuts on top. Serve at once, or cover and refrigerate until needed.

rainbow rotini salad

serves 4

This gorgeous salad with its intriguing combination of ingredients is an ideal candidate for a potluck—you're guaranteed to get rave reviews and recipe requests. It also makes a wonderful main dish salad at home. For extra protein, toss in some home-cooked or canned chickpeas or white beans. If tricolor rotini is unavailable, use regular rotini or another bite-size pasta.

8 ounces tricolor rotini pasta
1 cup shredded red cabbage
1 cup shredded green cabbage
1 large carrot, shredded
½ red bell pepper, cut into thin strips
½ cup chopped celery
½ cup dried sweetened cranberries
½ cup pistachios

½ cup pitted kalamata olives, halved
3 tablespoons minced scallions
3 tablespoons chopped fresh parsley
3 tablespoons olive oil
1½ tablespoons white wine vinegar
1 teaspoon sugar
½ teaspoon salt
¼ teaspoon freshly ground black pepper

Cook the rotini in a pot of boiling salted water until just tender. Drain, run under cold water, and transfer to a large bowl. Add the red cabbage, green cabbage, carrot, bell pepper, celery, cranberries, pistachios, olives, scallions, and parsley, and set aside. In a small bowl, combine the oil, vinegar, sugar, salt, and pepper, and mix well. Pour the dressing onto the salad, tossing well to coat and mix well. Taste and adjust the seasonings. Serve immediately, or cover and refrigerate until needed.

quinoa salad with apples and walnuts

serves 4

Quinoa is such a delicious protein-rich grain I'm always looking for more ways to enjoy it. Since I also like the Waldorf salad combo of apples, celery, and walnuts, this delicious salad was inevitable.

1 cup quinoa, thoroughly rinsed
2 Gala or Fuji apples, cored and chopped
2 teaspoons freshly squeezed lemon juice
½ cup chopped celery
½ cup walnut pieces, toasted (see page 17)
2 to 3 tablespoons minced red onion

¼ cup chopped fresh parsley
3 tablespoons olive oil
1½ tablespoons sherry vinegar
½ teaspoon sugar
½ teaspoon salt
¼ teaspoon freshly ground black pepper

Bring 2 cups of salted water to a boil. Add the quinoa, reduce the heat to low, cover, and simmer until the water is absorbed, 20 minutes. Drain any remaining water and blot the quinoa to remove excess moisture. Transfer to a serving bowl. While the quinoa is cooling, combine the apples and lemon juice in a large bowl and toss to coat. Add the celery, walnuts, onion, and parsley.

In a small bowl combine the oil, vinegar, sugar, salt, and pepper. Add the quinoa to the salad mixture and pour on the dressing. Toss well to combine. Taste and adjust the seasonings. Serve immediately, or cover and refrigerate until ready to use.

curried rice and chickpea salad

serves 4

Fresh, ripe diced mango adds its vibrant color and special sweetness to this tasty salad. When cutting the mango, save the juice that inevitably drips from the fruit to add to the dressing. If you have cooked rice on hand, here's an opportunity to use it. I especially like brown basmati in this salad.

1 ripe mango
3 cups cooked rice
1½ cups home-cooked chickpeas, or
   1 (15-ounce) can, drained and rinsed
1 red bell pepper, cut into ¼-inch dice
¼ cup minced scallions
⅓ cup golden raisins
⅓ cup roasted peanuts

2 tablespoons chopped fresh parsley or
   cilantro
2 tablespoons neutral vegetable oil
2 tablespoons mango juice
1 tablespoon rice vinegar
1 tablespoon curry powder, hot or mild
1 teaspoon sugar
1 teaspoon salt
⅛ teaspoon freshly ground black pepper

Slice through the mango lengthwise, next to one side of the flat pit, and detach; repeat for the other side. Spoon out the flesh, cut into ¼-inch dice, and transfer to a large bowl. Add the rice, chickpeas, bell pepper, scallions, raisins, peanuts, and parsley. Set aside.

In a small bowl, combine the oil, mango juice, vinegar, curry powder, sugar, salt, and pepper. Mix well, then pour the dressing onto the salad and toss gently to combine. Taste and adjust the seasonings. Serve immediately, or cover and refrigerate until needed.

sicilian-style orzo salad with walnuts and raisins

serves 4

The Sicilian penchant for combining sweet and savory flavors is evident in this salad that combines raisins with walnuts, olives, chickpeas, and a variety of vegetables. Tossed with orzo and a spicy vinaigrette, this zesty salad tastes even better if you set it aside at room temperature for 30 minutes to allow the flavors to blend. If you're not a fan of orzo, you can substitute another cooked pasta or grain. If you have a mini food processor, use that for the dressing to save cleanup time.

1 cup orzo

1½ cups home-cooked chickpeas, or
   1 (15-ounce) can, drained and rinsed

2 cups baby spinach, coarsely chopped

1 cup grape tomatoes, halved

3 scallions, minced

½ cup toasted walnut pieces (see page 17)

½ cup raisins

⅓ cup pitted kalamata olives, halved

⅓ cup coarsely chopped fresh basil leaves

3 large cloves garlic, crushed

1 shallot, halved

3 tablespoons olive oil

2 tablespoons white wine vinegar

½ teaspoon sugar

½ teaspoon red pepper flakes

½ teaspoon ground fennel seed

½ teaspoon salt

⅛ teaspoon freshly ground black pepper

Cook the orzo in a saucepan of boiling salted water until just tender, about 10 minutes. Drain and run under cold water, then transfer to a large bowl. Add the chickpeas, spinach, tomatoes, scallions, walnuts, raisins, olives, and basil. Set aside.

In a food processor, combine the garlic and shallot and process to a paste. Add the oil, vinegar, sugar, red pepper flakes, fennel, salt, and pepper. Process until well blended. Pour the dressing over the salad and toss gently to combine. Serve at once.

deconstructed báhn mì salad

serves 4

All the elements of a Vietnamese báhn mì sandwich are reconfigured for the salad bowl in this luscious main dish. My favorite sandwich is now my favorite salad, too! If you prefer less heat, cut back on the amount of sriracha sauce.

2 tablespoons neutral vegetable oil
8 ounces seitan or extra-firm tofu, thinly
    sliced
2 cloves garlic, minced
1½ teaspoons grated fresh ginger
3 tablespoons soy sauce
2 tablespoons hoisin sauce
2 teaspoons sriracha sauce
1 teaspoon sugar

2 tablespoons rice wine vinegar
3 cups finely shredded cabbage
1 large carrot, shredded
½ English cucumber, seeded and chopped
1 cup fresh cilantro leaves
¼ cup minced scallions
½ baguette, cut diagonally into ½-inch
    slices
Vegan mayonnaise

Heat the oil in a skillet over medium heat. Add the seitan and cook until browned on both sides, about 4 minutes per side. Add the garlic and ginger and cook until fragrant, 1 minute longer. Splash with 1 tablespoon of the soy sauce and set aside to cool.

In a small bowl, combine the remaining 2 tablespoons soy sauce with the hoisin, sriracha, sugar, and vinegar, stirring well to blend. Set aside.

Spread the cabbage on a large platter, sprinkle evenly with the carrot, cucumber, cilantro, and scallions. Arrange the seitan on top and drizzle with the reserved sauce.

Toast the baguette slices and spread with a thin layer of vegan mayonnaise. Arrange the bread around the outside of the salad platter and serve immediately.

green papaya and tofu salad

serves 4

Shredded papaya shares the stage with tofu in this refreshing and spicy salad. The papaya salads served in Thai restaurants often contain shrimp and are seasoned with fish sauce. Now you can enjoy this salad at home.

1 tablespoon neutral vegetable oil
8 ounces extra-firm tofu, drained and cut into ½-inch dice
1½ tablespoons soy sauce
2 tablespoons toasted sesame oil
2 tablespoons minced red onion
2 tablespoons mango or orange juice
2 tablespoons rice wine vinegar
2 teaspoons grated fresh ginger

½ teaspoon red pepper flakes
½ teaspoon sugar
Salt and freshly ground black pepper
1 large green papaya, shredded (about 3 cups)
3 cups shredded lettuce
1 carrot, grated or shredded
6 grape tomatoes, halved
⅓ cup crushed peanuts

Heat the oil in a nonstick skillet over medium-high heat. Add the tofu and cook until golden brown all over, 5 to 7 minutes. Add 1 tablespoon of the soy sauce and cook, stirring to coat. Remove from the heat and set aside.

In a bowl, combine the sesame oil, onion, mango juice, vinegar, the remaining ½ tablespoon soy sauce, the ginger, red pepper flakes, sugar, and salt and pepper to taste. Stir to mix well. Add the papaya and toss gently to combine.

To assemble, arrange the shredded lettuce on a platter or individual salad plates. Use a pair of tongs to top with the papaya, letting any excess dressing drain back into the bowl. Top the papaya with the reserved tofu and sprinkle with the grated carrot. Garnish with the tomatoes and drizzle with any remaining dressing. Sprinkle with the peanuts and serve immediately.

spicy red bean slaw

serves 4

The addition of red beans and corn transforms a side of slaw into a great main dish salad. If you can find bagged shredded cabbage, this speedy salad will go together even more quickly.

3 cups finely shredded cabbage
1½ cups home-cooked red beans, or
   1 (15-ounce) can, drained and rinsed
1½ cups fresh or thawed frozen corn
   kernels
2 chipotle chiles in adobo, finely minced
¼ cup minced red onion
¼ cup chopped fresh cilantro

2 cloves garlic, crushed
1 teaspoon ground cumin
½ teaspoon salt
¼ teaspoon freshly ground black pepper
1 teaspoon sugar
2 tablespoons freshly squeezed lime juice
1 tablespoon cider vinegar
¼ cup olive oil

In a large bowl, combine the cabbage, beans, corn, chiles, onion, and cilantro. Set aside.

In a blender or food processor, mince the garlic with the cumin, salt, pepper, and sugar. Add the lime juice, vinegar, and oil and process until blended. Pour the dressing onto the slaw and toss to combine. Taste and adjust the seasonings. Serve at once.

farmers' market pasta salad

serves 4 to 6

Inspired by the abundance of vegetables on my kitchen counter after a trip to the farmers' market, this versatile salad can be varied according to whatever veggies you have on hand. For example, use any color bell pepper, substitute yellow summer squash for the zucchini, or leave out the fennel if you don't have it.

8 ounces farfalle or other bite-size pasta

3 tablespoons olive oil

5 cloves garlic, minced

5 scallions, minced

1 yellow bell pepper, diced

1 small zucchini, halved lengthwise and thinly sliced

3 cups baby spinach

Salt and freshly ground black pepper

1½ cups grape tomatoes, halved lengthwise

1 small fennel bulb, quartered and thinly sliced

1½ cups home-cooked cannellini beans, or 1 (15-ounce) can, drained and rinsed

½ cup pitted kalamata olives, halved

⅓ cup fresh basil leaves

¼ cup fresh parsley leaves

2 tablespoons rice vinegar

½ teaspoon sugar

Cook the farfalle in a pot of boiling salted water until just tender, about 10 minutes. Drain and rinse under cold water, then transfer to a large bowl. Set aside.

Heat the oil in a skillet over medium heat. Add the garlic and cook until softened, 1 minute. Add the scallions, bell pepper, zucchini, and spinach. Cook just long enough to remove the raw taste from the vegetables, 2 to 3 minutes. Season to taste with salt and pepper and transfer to the bowl with the pasta.

Add the tomatoes, fennel, beans, olives, basil, and parsley. Sprinkle on the vinegar and sugar, and salt and pepper to taste. Toss gently to mix well. Serve at once.

corn, red bean, and blueberry salad with mango dressing

serves 4

If it's true that we eat first with our eyes, you'll devour this colorful salad in seconds. But it's more than just pretty—this luscious salad tastes great too. The small amount of sriracha in the dressing adds more flavor dimension than heat. If you prefer it a little spicier, double the sriracha.

MANGO DRESSING
3 tablespoons mango juice or mango puree
2 tablespoons freshly squeezed lime juice
1 tablespoon agave nectar, or 1 teaspoon
   sugar
½ teaspoon sriracha sauce
¼ teaspoon salt

SALAD
1 ripe mango
2 cups corn kernels
2 cups blueberries
1½ cups home-cooked dark red kidney
   beans, or 1 (15-ounce) can, drained
   and rinsed
1 cucumber, seeded and chopped
1 carrot, shredded
3 tablespoons minced scallions
¼ cup fresh cilantro, parsley, basil, or
   tarragon leaves
3 cups mixed baby lettuce

To make the dressing, in a small bowl, combine the mango juice, lime juice, agave, sriracha, and salt. Stir to blend. Set aside.

For the salad, slice through the mango lengthwise, next to one side of the flat pit, and detach; repeat for the other side. Spoon out the flesh, chop, and transfer to a large bowl. Add the corn, blueberries, kidney beans, cucumber, carrot, scallions, and cilantro. Pour the dressing over the salad and toss gently to combine. Serve on a bed of mixed lettuce. Serve at once.

romaine and pear salad with sherry-walnut vinaigrette

serves 4

This easy and elegant salad is made with crisp romaine lettuce and juicy ripe pears. Toasted walnuts add crunch, and a luxurious vinaigrette made with walnut oil and sherry vinegar unifies the flavors.

SHERRY-WALNUT VINAIGRETTE
2½ tablespoons sherry vinegar
1 small clove garlic, crushed in a garlic
   press
½ teaspoon dried tarragon
½ teaspoon dried basil
½ teaspoon sugar
½ teaspoon salt

⅛ teaspoon freshly ground black pepper
2 tablespoons walnut oil
2 tablespoons neutral vegetable oil

1 head romaine lettuce, torn into bite-size
   pieces
1 or 2 ripe Bosc pears, cored and chopped
⅓ cup toasted walnut pieces (see page 17)

To make the vinaigrette, in a small bowl, combine the vinegar, garlic, tarragon, basil, sugar, salt, and pepper. Stir in the walnut oil and the vegetable oil until well blended. Set aside.

In a large bowl, combine the lettuce, pears, and walnuts. Drizzle on the dressing and toss well to coat. Serve immediately.

wilted cabbage salad with creamy balsamic dressing

serves 4

Lovely red cabbage, the star of this delicious salad, is slightly softened by a quick sauté with shallots and cashews, then tossed with a creamy dressing. The optional seitan adds protein for a more substantial variation. The versatile dressing is also great on simple tossed salads or tossed with roasted vegetables such as Brussels sprouts, cauliflower, or asparagus.

1 tablespoon olive oil
2 shallots, thinly sliced
6 cups shredded red cabbage (about
    1½ pounds)
6 ounces seitan, cut into strips (optional)
⅓ cup roasted unsalted cashews
⅓ cup dried cranberries

CREAMY BALSAMIC DRESSING
2 cloves garlic, crushed
2 scallions, minced
½ teaspoon salt
3 tablespoons tahini
2 tablespoons balsamic vinegar, white or
    brown (see note)
2 tablespoons freshly squeezed lemon juice
½ teaspoon sugar
¼ teaspoon freshly ground black pepper
2 tablespoons olive oil

Heat the oil in a large skillet over medium-high heat. Add the shallots, then add the cabbage and seitan, if using, and stir-fry until the cabbage is slightly softened, 8 to 10 minutes. Add the cashews and cranberries and stir-fry to combine and heat through, 2 minutes. Remove from the heat and set aside.

To make the dressing, grind the garlic, scallions, and salt in a blender or food processor. Add the tahini, vinegar, lemon juice, sugar, pepper, and olive oil, and process until smooth.

Transfer the cabbage mixture to a large bowl and drizzle with enough of the dressing to coat. Toss to combine and serve immediately.

note: Regular balsamic vinegar lends a dark tint to this dressing. If you prefer a dressing that is lighter in color, use white balsamic vinegar—the dressing is delicious either way.

easy make-ahead bakes

These make-ahead recipes are for times when you come home late and don't feel like cooking. Just bake and serve—and no messy cleanup. Although the recipes in this chapter require baking, they conform to the less than 30 minutes of active time rule and are designed to be quickly assembled ahead of time. That way, you can either bake them immediately or refrigerate them for later use. Of course, it's also fun to prepare oven-baked meals on cold days so the heat of the oven can warm you up while the fragrance of dinner baking fills the house.

Enjoy global flavors with recipes such as Sicilian Stuffed Shells, Cajun-Spiced Dirty Rice, and Moroccan Vegetable Packets. With three different sauce options, the Snowballs in Hell are as delicious as they are whimsical. Kids of all ages will love the Mac and Cheezeburger Bake, and the two sensational pizza recipes will turn your kitchen into a gourmet pizzeria. Many of these dishes, such as the Indian Shepherd's Pie or Tuscan Kale Lasagne, make great company fare as well.

NOTE: These recipes lend themselves to assembling in advance, then refrigerating and baking when ready to use. When baking a dish that has been refrigerated, let it come to room temperature before baking. Otherwise, allow an additional 15 to 20 minutes of baking to be sure the center is hot.

mac and cheezeburger bake

serves 6

baking time: 30 minutes

This recipe has "comfort food" written all over it. Even picky eaters will enjoy this satisfying take on mac and cheese made hearty with the addition of minced seitan. Add some cooked chopped broccoli for a complete meal in one baking dish.

8 ounces elbow macaroni
1 tablespoon olive oil
8 ounces finely minced seitan (see note)
1 tablespoon soy sauce
1 cup firm tofu, drained
1½ cups unsweetened nondairy milk
1¼ cups vegetable broth
½ cup nutritional yeast
2 tablespoons cornstarch

2 tablespoons freshly squeezed lemon juice
1 teaspoon prepared yellow mustard
1 teaspoon salt
1 teaspoon garlic powder
1 teaspoon onion powder
¼ teaspoon ground turmeric
¼ teaspoon freshly ground black pepper
⅓ cup panko or fresh bread crumbs

Cook the macaroni in a pot of boiling salted water until al dente, 7 to 9 minutes. While the pasta is cooking, heat the oil in a skillet over medium heat. Add the seitan and cook until browned, about 7 minutes. Add the soy sauce, stirring to coat. Remove from the heat and set aside.

In a food processor, process the tofu until smooth. Add the nondairy milk, broth, nutritional yeast, cornstarch, lemon juice, mustard, salt, garlic powder, onion powder, turmeric, and pepper. Blend until smooth.

Preheat the oven to 375°F. Lightly oil a large baking dish and set aside. Drain the cooked macaroni and return it to the pot. Add the reserved seitan and the sauce mixture and mix well. Taste and adjust the seasonings, adding more salt if needed. Transfer the mixture to the prepared baking dish, top with the bread crumbs, and bake until hot and the crumbs are nicely browned, about 30 minutes. Serve hot.

note: For the seitan, you can substitute crumbled sautéed tempeh, vegan burger crumbles, or three chopped "meaty" vegan burgers.

pecan-crusted
maple-mustard seitan

serves 4

baking time: 20 minutes

A luscious coating of maple, mustard, and ground pecans transforms seitan into an elegant main dish. The pecans should be finely ground, almost to a coarse meal. For an easy meal that's fancy enough for company, serve with freshly cooked quinoa and roasted asparagus or Brussels sprouts.

1 cup very finely ground pecans (4 ounces)
⅓ cup pure maple syrup
3 tablespoons brown mustard

2 tablespoons soy sauce
12 ounces seitan, thinly sliced

Line a baking sheet with parchment paper or lightly oil the baking sheet and set aside. Preheat the oven to 375°F.

In a shallow bowl, combine the pecans, maple syrup, mustard, and soy sauce. Mix until combined. Dip the seitan into the mixture to coat well.

Arrange the seitan on the prepared baking sheet and bake until nicely browned, 10 minutes. Remove from the oven, carefully turn the seitan over, and return to the oven to bake until browned on the other side, another 10 minutes. Serve hot.

portobellos stuffed with chickpeas and chard

serves 4

baking time: 25 minutes

Large portobello mushroom caps make a terrific main dish when stuffed with a flavorful filling of chickpeas and chard seasoned with garlic, ginger, soy sauce, and sesame oil. Sprinkle panko crumbs on top for a crunchy finish. To complete the meal, put on a pot of quinoa or a quick-cooking rice such as basmati when you begin this recipe, and your grain will be ready by the time the mushrooms are done baking.

4 large portobello mushroom caps,
   stems and gills removed
1 tablespoon olive oil
¼ cup minced onion
3 cloves garlic, minced
1 teaspoon grated fresh ginger
1 bunch chard, finely chopped

2 tablespoons soy sauce
2 teaspoons toasted sesame oil
1½ cups home-cooked chickpeas, or
   1 (15-ounce) can, drained and rinsed
¾ cup panko crumbs, plus more for
   topping
Salt and freshly ground black pepper

Preheat the oven to 400°F. Arrange the mushroom caps, stem side up, in a lightly oiled baking dish and set aside. Heat the olive oil in a skillet over medium-high heat. Add the onion, garlic, ginger, and chard. Drizzle on the soy sauce and sesame oil and cook until the onion is soft and the chard is tender, about 7 minutes. Set aside.

Mash the chickpeas in a bowl. Drain off and reserve any liquid from the chard mixture. Add the chard mixture to the chickpeas and mix well to combine. Add the ¾ cup panko and season to taste with salt and pepper. Mix well. Spoon the stuffing mixture into the mushroom caps. Drizzle any remaining chard liquid around the mushrooms and top with additional panko, if desired. Cover and bake for 15 minutes, then uncover and bake until the mushrooms are tender and the stuffing is hot, about 10 minutes. Serve hot.

tuscan vegetable tart

serves 4

baking time: 25 minutes

This simple and delicious tart, with its flaky brown crust and colorful vegetables, looks more time-consuming than it is. A creamy white bean layer binds it all together and adds protein for a lovely main dish. A crisp green salad completes the meal.

1 sheet frozen vegan puff pastry, thawed
1 tablespoon olive oil
1 zucchini, halved lengthwise and thinly sliced
1 cup cremini mushrooms, thinly sliced
4 scallions, minced
3 cloves garlic, minced
1 cup grape tomatoes, halved lengthwise
1 roasted red bell pepper (see page 16), cut into 1-inch pieces
3 tablespoons fresh basil, chopped

1 teaspoon dried marjoram
½ teaspoon salt
¼ teaspoon freshly ground black pepper
1½ cups home-cooked cannellini beans, or 1 (15-ounce) can, drained and rinsed
1 tablespoon white wine vinegar or freshly squeezed lemon juice
2 teaspoons capers
2 tablespoons chopped fresh parsley
2 tablespoons nutritional yeast
¼ cup ground pine nuts

Preheat the oven to 400°F. Press the pastry sheet into a 9-inch tart pan or pie plate, crimping and trimming the edges to fit. Pierce the bottom of the pastry with a fork and bake until golden, 10 to 12 minutes. Set aside to cool. Lightly oil a large shallow baking dish. Reduce the oven temperature to 375°F.

While the crust is baking, heat the oil in a large skillet over medium-high heat. Add the zucchini, mushrooms, scallions, and garlic. Cook, stirring, until softened, about 4 minutes. Add the tomatoes, bell pepper, basil, marjoram, salt, and pepper. Stir to mix well, then remove from the heat.

Mash the white beans, vinegar, and capers in a bowl. Stir in the parsley and nutritional yeast, and mix well to combine. Spread the bean mixture in the bottom of the reserved crust. Spread the vegetables evenly over the bean mixture, then sprinkle the top with the pine nuts. Bake until the vegetables are hot and the crust is nicely browned, 15 to 20 minutes. Serve hot.

jambalaya bake

serves 4

baking time: 1 hour

Try this recipe if you enjoy the spicy rich flavor of jambalaya but don't have time to tend to a slow simmering pot on the stove. Just a few minutes of prep and it's ready to go into the oven to finish cooking. I use a basmati rice in this because it cooks fairly quickly, but any quick-cooking brown or white rice may be used. (If you use regular brown rice, you'll need to increase the cooking time.) Diced seitan or tempeh may be substituted for the vegan sausage. A minced fresh jalapeño may be used instead of canned chiles.

2 tablespoons olive oil
8 ounces vegan sausage links, cut into ¼-inch slices
1 yellow onion, chopped
1 green bell pepper, chopped
1 celery rib, chopped
3 cloves garlic, minced
1 cup brown basmati rice or quick-cooking brown rice
1 (28-ounce) can diced tomatoes, including juice

1½ cups home-cooked dark red kidney beans, or 1 (15-ounce) can, drained and rinsed
1 (4-ounce) can chopped green chiles, hot or mild, drained
2 cups vegetable broth
1 teaspoon dried marjoram, or ½ teaspoon dried oregano
1 teaspoon salt
¼ teaspoon freshly ground black pepper
Tabasco sauce

Preheat the oven to 375°F. Lightly oil a 3-quart baking dish and set aside.

In a skillet, heat 1 tablespoon of the oil over medium heat. Add the vegan sausage and cook until browned, stirring occasionally, about 5 minutes. Remove from the skillet and transfer to the prepared baking dish. Set aside.

Heat the remaining 1 tablespoon oil in the same skillet. Add the onion, bell pepper, celery, and garlic. Cover and cook until softened, about 7 minutes, then add to the baking dish with the sausage. Stir in the rice, tomatoes, beans, chiles, broth, marjoram, salt, pepper, and Tabasco to taste. Cover tightly and bake until the rice and vegetables are tender, about 1 hour. Serve hot.

sicilian stuffed shells

serves 4

baking time: 30 minutes

In addition to being a terrific make-ahead dish, stuffed shells are great when company's coming. Everyone loves pasta, and the shells look and feel more special than regular pasta and are much easier to serve than lasagne. The filling in this recipe contains the Sicilian trademark touch of raisins which lend a slight sweetness to the dish. (You can leave them out if anyone in your crowd is raisin averse.) Serve with a crisp green salad.

12 large pasta shells
3 cloves garlic, crushed
1 cup walnut pieces
½ cup chopped fresh Italian parsley
⅓ cup golden raisins
½ teaspoon red pepper flakes
½ teaspoon ground fennel seed

12 ounces firm tofu, well drained
2 tablespoons nutritional yeast
1 teaspoon salt
¼ teaspoon freshly ground black pepper
3 cups marinara sauce
¼ cup vegan Parmesan (optional)

Preheat the oven to 350°F. Cook the pasta shells in a large pot of boiling salted water, stirring occasionally, until al dente, about 8 minutes. Drain the pasta shells and run under cold water. Set aside.

In a food processor, combine the garlic, walnuts, parsley, raisins, red pepper flakes, and fennel, and pulse until finely minced and well combined. Mash the tofu in a bowl with the nutritional yeast, salt, and pepper. Add the garlic and walnut mixture and mix well to thoroughly combine.

Spread a thin layer of the marinara sauce on the bottom of a 9 by 13-inch baking dish. Use a teaspoon to stuff the filling into the shells until well packed. Arrange the stuffed shells on the sauce in the baking dish, and pour the remaining sauce over the shells. Cover tightly with foil and bake until hot, about 30 minutes. To serve, sprinkle with the vegan Parmesan, if desired, and serve hot.

cajun-spiced dirty rice

serves 4

baking time: 50 minutes

The New Orleans vegetable trinity of onion, bell pepper, and celery combined with Cajun spices provides the flavor in this zesty rice casserole, while mushrooms are used instead of the traditional meat. For added flavor, include some chopped sautéed vegan sausage sprinkled with Cajun spices. A quick-cooking brown rice is used for faster baking, but a basmati rice is good here as well. If using a regular long-grain brown rice, you'll need to cook it much longer and may also need to add a little more liquid.

INGREDIENT ALERT: Check the salt level of your Cajun spice blend and vegetable broth before adding additional salt.

1 tablespoon olive oil
1 onion, minced
1 celery rib, minced
1 green bell pepper, minced

4 cloves garlic, minced
8 ounces mushrooms, finely chopped
2 teaspoons Cajun spice blend
1 cup quick-cooking brown rice
1½ cups home-cooked red beans, or
   1 (15-ounce) can, drained and rinsed
2 cups vegetable broth
Salt and freshly ground black pepper

Preheat the oven to 375°F. Lightly oil a 3-quart baking dish and set aside. Heat the oil in a skillet over medium heat. Add the onion, celery, and bell pepper. Cover and cook to soften, 5 minutes. Add the garlic, mushrooms, and Cajun spices. Stir to combine and cook until softened, 2 minutes. Transfer the mixture to the prepared baking dish. Stir in the rice, beans, broth, and salt and pepper to taste. Cover tightly and cook until the rice is tender, about 50 minutes. Serve hot.

moroccan vegetable packets

serves 4

baking time: 20 minutes

These delectable packets may seem fussy, but they're not, thanks to frozen vegan puff pastry. Chopping the vegetables is the most time-consuming part. If you have a Moroccan spice blend, you can use that in place of all the spices. Once assembled, the packets take just 20 minutes to bake. You can also cut the pastry into smaller pieces and make several little appetizers instead of four large dinner-size packets.

1 tablespoon olive oil
1 small yellow onion, chopped
1 small red bell pepper, chopped
1 small carrot, shredded
1 small zucchini, chopped
3 to 4 cloves garlic, minced
½ teaspoon ground coriander
½ teaspoon ground ginger
¼ teaspoon ground allspice
¼ teaspoon ground cinnamon

¼ teaspoon ground cumin
¼ teaspoon ground turmeric
¼ teaspoon cayenne
½ teaspoon salt
1½ cups home-cooked chickpeas, or
   1 (15-ounce) can, rinsed and drained
1 (14.5-ounce) can diced tomatoes, well
   drained
1 tablespoon freshly squeezed lemon juice
1 sheet frozen vegan puff pastry, thawed

Heat the oil in a large skillet over medium heat. Add the onion, cover, and cook until softened, 4 minutes. Add the bell pepper, carrot, zucchini, garlic, coriander, ginger, allspice, cinnamon, cumin, turmeric, cayenne, and salt. Cook, stirring, until tender, 5 to 6 minutes. Stir in the chickpeas, tomatoes, and lemon juice. Cook, stirring, to blend the flavors and evaporate any liquid, about 5 minutes. Remove from the heat to cool, mashing some of the chickpeas with a fork. Taste and adjust the seasonings. Drain any remaining liquid that may occur as the mixture cools.

Preheat the oven to 400°F. Roll out the pastry on a lightly floured surface. Cut into 4 equal pieces. Spoon the filling mixture evenly onto each piece of pastry, then fold one end of the pastry over the filling to meet the opposite end of the dough. Use your fingers to seal and pinch the edges to enclose the filling. Pierce the top of the pastry with a fork and arrange the packets on an ungreased baking sheet. Bake until golden brown, about 20 minutes. Serve hot.

tuscan kale lasagne

serves 6 to 8

baking time: 45 minutes

Nutritious and flavorful Tuscan kale, also known as dinosaur, black, or lacinato kale, is a welcome inclusion in this lasagne, adding a wonderful texture and color element, and also making this a one-dish meal. If unavailable, another dark leafy green such as chard or spinach may be substituted.

1 box lasagna noodles (12 noodles)
2 pounds extra-firm tofu, well drained
   and mashed
½ cup nutritional yeast
¼ cup chopped fresh parsley
1 tablespoon freshly squeezed lemon juice
1½ teaspoons dried basil
½ teaspoon ground fennel seed
½ teaspoon dried oregano

Salt and freshly ground black pepper
2 tablespoons olive oil
2 shallots, minced
3 large cloves garlic, minced
8 ounces Tuscan kale, finely chopped
6 ounces cremini mushrooms, chopped
4 cups marinara sauce
⅓ cup ground pine nuts

Preheat the oven to 350°F. Place the noodles in a large shallow baking dish and add enough boiling water to cover. Set aside while you make the filling.

In a large bowl, combine the tofu and nutritional yeast. Mash well to combine. Add the parsley, lemon juice, basil, fennel, oregano, 1 teaspoon salt, and ½ teaspoon pepper. Mix well to combine. Taste and adjust the seasonings.

Heat the oil in a skillet over medium heat. Add the shallots and garlic and cook until softened, 3 minutes. Add the kale and season with salt. Cook until wilted, about 3 minutes. Add the mushrooms and cook until softened and any liquid is absorbed, 5 minutes. Set aside.

Drain and blot the noodles. Spread a layer of the marinara sauce in the bottom of a 9 by 13-inch baking pan. Arrange 4 of the noodles on top of the sauce, overlapping slightly. Spread half of the tofu mixture over the noodles in a thin layer. Spread half of the kale mixture. Repeat layering with the sauce, noodles, the remaining tofu mixture, and the remaining kale mixture, ending with the noodles topped with the marinara sauce. Top with the pine nuts. Cover the lasagne with foil until hot throughout, 45 minutes. Let stand for at least 10 minutes before serving.

indian shepherd's pie

serves 4 to 6

baking time: 30 minutes

Shepherd's pie goes from everyday to exotic with this Indian-inspired twist. A creamy potato-cauliflower topping and curried bean and vegetable filling give this savory casserole a samosa-like flavor that is out-of-this-world delicious.

2 russet potatoes, diced
2 cups cauliflower florets
2 tablespoons vegan butter
Salt and freshly ground black pepper
1 tablespoon olive oil
1 yellow onion, finely chopped
2 carrots, chopped
2 tablespoons curry powder

1½ cups home-cooked dark red kidney beans, or 1 (15-ounce) can, drained and rinsed
1 cup frozen peas, thawed
3 cups fresh baby spinach, chopped
1 (14-ounce) can diced tomatoes, well drained
1 cup unsweetened coconut milk

Steam the potatoes and cauliflower over boiling water until tender, about 15 minutes. Mash the potatoes and cauliflower with the butter, and salt and pepper to taste. Set aside. Preheat the oven to 350°F. Lightly oil a shallow baking dish and set aside.

Heat the oil in a skillet over medium heat. Add the onion and carrots, cover, and cook until soft, 5 minutes. Stir in the curry powder and cook until fragrant, 30 seconds. Transfer to the prepared baking dish. Add the beans, peas, spinach, tomatoes, and coconut milk. Season to taste with salt and pepper. Stir to combine. Spread the reserved potato and cauliflower mixture evenly on top. Bake until hot, about 30 minutes. Serve hot.

roasted ratatouille

serves 4 to 6

baking time: 30 minutes

The classic vegetable stew of France just got better thanks to the miracle of roasting, which deliciously intensifies the flavors of the vegetables. It's especially good served with warm crusty bread.

1 yellow onion, chopped
2 zucchini, halved lengthwise and cut into
   ¼-inch slices
1 red bell pepper, chopped
1 eggplant, cut into ½-inch dice
2 cups cherry tomatoes
5 cloves garlic, chopped
1 teaspoon dried marjoram

1 teaspoon dried thyme
1 teaspoon dried basil
½ teaspoon dried oregano
Salt and freshly ground black pepper
2 tablespoons olive oil
2 tablespoons torn fresh basil leaves
2 tablespoons chopped fresh parsley

Preheat the oven to 425°F. In a large bowl, combine the onion, zucchini, bell pepper, eggplant, tomatoes, and garlic. Sprinkle on the marjoram, thyme, dried basil, and oregano and season generously with salt and pepper. Drizzle on the oil and toss to combine. Spread the vegetable mixture into a large baking pan. Roast until the vegetables are tender but not mushy, turning once, about 30 minutes. To serve, transfer to a serving bowl, sprinkle with the fresh basil and parsley, and taste to adjust the seasonings. Serve hot.

autumn harvest gratin

serves 4

baking time: 65 minutes

I like to make this gratin when the first chill of autumn sets in and the welcome fragrance of baking vegetables fills the house. The gratin combines white and sweet potatoes with carrots and parsnips, along with end-of-summer favorites: fennel, tomato, and bell pepper. A light sprinkling of pecans on top adds texture and flavor.

2 tablespoons olive oil
1 yellow onion, minced (1 cup)
1 yellow bell pepper, minced (⅔ cup)
3 cloves garlic, minced
1 teaspoon dried thyme
1 teaspoon dried basil
½ teaspoon dried sage
½ cup vegetable broth
Salt and freshly ground black pepper

1 ripe tomato, diced (¾ cup)
1 large sweet potato, thinly sliced (3 cups)
1 large russet potato, thinly sliced
   (2⅓ cups)
1 fennel bulb, thinly sliced (3 cups)
1 carrot, thinly sliced (½ cup)
1 parsnip, thinly sliced (¾ cup)
⅓ cup ground pecans

Preheat the oven to 400°F. Lightly oil a 1½ quart gratin dish or shallow baking dish and set aside. Heat 1 tablespoon of the oil in a skillet over medium heat. Add the onion, bell pepper, and garlic. Sprinkle on the thyme, basil, and sage. Cover, and cook to soften, about 5 minutes. Stir in the broth and season to taste with salt and pepper. Transfer the mixture to a blender or food processor, add the tomato, and process until smooth. Taste and adjust the seasonings.

In the prepared gratin dish, arrange layers of the sweet potato, russet potato, fennel, carrot, and parsnip, overlapping and seasoning lightly with salt and pepper as you layer the vegetables. Pour on the reserved onion mixture. Cover tightly with aluminum foil and bake until the vegetables are tender, about 55 minutes. Uncover, sprinkle with pecans, and bake uncovered for 10 minutes longer to toast the pecans. Serve hot.

special spicy empanadas

baking time: 20 minutes

What's so special? Unlike most empanada recipes, this one uses frozen puff pastry for the dough and a luscious sweet potato and pinto bean filling. To save time (and a pot) you can bake the whole (unpeeled) sweet potato in the microwave for 5 minutes or until tender, then peel and chop. If you have a leftover baked potato (white or sweet), you can use it instead of steaming a potato.

1 small sweet potato, chopped (about ¾ cup)

2 teaspoons olive oil

1 small yellow onion, chopped

3 cloves garlic, minced

1 teaspoon chili powder

½ teaspoon ground cumin

½ teaspoon dried oregano

½ teaspoon salt

¼ teaspoon freshly ground black pepper

1 cup home-cooked pinto beans, or canned beans, drained and rinsed

¼ cup frozen corn kernels, thawed

1 tablespoon minced chipotle chile in adobo

2 tablespoons sliced pimiento-stuffed green olives (optional)

1 sheet frozen vegan puff pastry, thawed

Steam the sweet potato over boiling water until tender, about 8 minutes. Set aside.

Heat the oil in a skillet over medium heat. Add the onion, cover, and cook until tender, 5 minutes. Add the garlic and cook until fragrant. Stir in the chili powder, cumin, oregano, salt, and pepper. Mix well to combine. Set aside.

In a large bowl, mash the pinto beans, then add the corn, chile, and olives, if using. Stir in the onion mixture and the sweet potato and mix well to combine. Set aside to cool.

Preheat the oven to 400°F. Roll out the pastry on a lightly floured work surface and divide into four equal pieces, each 5 to 6 inches square.

Spoon the filling evenly onto each dough piece, then fold one end of the dough over the filling to meet the opposite end of the dough. Use your fingers to seal and pinch the edges to enclose the filling. Pierce the top of the pastry with a fork and place the empanadas on an ungreased baking sheet. Bake until golden brown, about 20 minutes.

tempeh normandy

serves 4

baking time: 30 minutes

A delectable creamy sauce made with apple brandy and soy creamer elevates tempeh to company fare in this Normandy-style dish made with apples. According to recipe testers, you may want to double the recipe because you're bound to want seconds. I like to serve it over brown basmati rice, which can be prepared ahead of time or cooked while the tempeh bakes.

1 tablespoon olive oil
12 ounces tempeh, cut into 1-inch dice
3 shallots, minced
8 ounces white mushrooms, sliced
1 large cooking apple, cored and thinly sliced
1 tablespoon all-purpose flour
½ cup apple cider or apple juice

¼ cup apple brandy (or more cider or apple juice)
1 teaspoon dried thyme
Salt and freshly ground black pepper
⅓ cup unflavored soy creamer
¼ cup chopped toasted walnuts (see page 17)
2 tablespoons chopped fresh parsley

Preheat the oven to 350°F. Heat the oil in an ovenproof skillet over medium heat. Add the tempeh and cook until browned, about 5 minutes. Remove from the skillet, and set aside. In the same skillet, add the shallots and mushrooms and cook for 2 to 3 minutes. Add the apple and cook until softened, 2 minutes. Stir in the flour and cook for 1 minute to remove the raw taste.

Stir in the cider, brandy, and thyme, and bring to a boil. Return the tempeh to the skillet. Season to taste with salt and pepper. Cover and bake until hot, 30 minutes.

Remove from the oven and spoon about half the sauce mixture (including some of the apple, mushrooms, and shallots, but not the tempeh) into a blender or food processor. Add the soy creamer and process until smooth, then return the sauce to the pan and heat until warm. To serve, arrange the tempeh on plates and spoon the sauce on top. Sprinkle with walnuts and parsley. Serve hot.

note: If you use apple juice instead of brandy, the end result will be a bit sweeter, but nonetheless delicious.

muffuletta pizza

serves 4

baking time: 15 minutes

A muffuletta is a popular New Orleans sandwich named for the round Italian bread loaf in which it is traditionally made. The hallmark of the sandwich is a piquant olive salad which is part of the filling. This recipe incorporates the flavors of a muffuletta sandwich into a gorgeous pizza that would be great served as an appetizer or for lunch. If serving for dinner, accompany it with a tossed green salad. Ready-to-use pizza dough (available in most supermarkets) gets this pizza in the oven in minutes. To save time, substitute 1 cup (or more) of prepared Italian olive salad or giardiniera for the topping ingredients; both are available at Italian grocers and some supermarkets or online.

Pizza dough for 1 crust, at room temperature, store-bought or homemade (see page 15)
1½ cups home-cooked chickpeas, or
   1 (15-ounce) can, drained and rinsed
2 cloves garlic, crushed
2 teaspoons freshly squeezed lemon juice
1 teaspoon chopped fresh oregano, or
   ½ teaspoon dried
2 tablespoons vegan mayonnaise
½ teaspoon Dijon mustard
½ teaspoon Tabasco sauce
Salt and freshly ground black pepper

1 (6-ounce) jar marinated artichoke hearts,
   drained and sliced
1 small ripe Hass avocado
½ cup pimiento-stuffed green olives,
   coarsely chopped
⅓ cup pitted kalamata olives, coarsely
   chopped
2 teaspoons capers
2 scallions, minced
2 tablespoons chopped fresh parsley

Position the oven rack on the lowest level of the oven, and preheat the oven to 425°F.

Spread the crust onto a pizza pan, stretching to fit. Set aside.

In a food processor, combine the chickpeas, garlic, lemon juice, oregano, mayonnaise, mustard, Tabasco, and salt and pepper to taste. Process until smooth. Spread the mixture evenly onto the pizza crust, to within ½ inch of the edge. Arrange the artichoke slices evenly on top of the pizza. Bake on the lowest oven rack until the crust is golden brown, about 15 minutes.

While the pizza is baking, halve and pit the avocado, spoon out the flesh, chop, and transfer to a bowl. Add the green olives, kalamata olives, capers, scallions, and parsley and combine. Season to taste with salt and pepper and mix well to combine. When the pizza comes out of the oven, top evenly with the olive mixture and serve hot.

variation: For a more traditional pizza, eliminate the pizza toppings in the recipe and instead top the dough with a thin layer of prepared pizza sauce and sprinkle with vegan cheese, then bake as directed.

antipasto pizza

baking time: 15 minutes

Topped with a variety of ingredients found in a supermarket olive bar, this loaded pizza features many of the flavors in an Italian antipasto. It makes an easy weeknight dinner when served with a tossed green salad.

Whether you use the pizza dough on page 15 or ready-to-use pizza dough from the supermarket, bring it to room temperature before using so it stretches more easily, allowing you to get the pizza in the oven in minutes.

Pizza dough for 1 crust, store-bought or homemade (see page 15), at room temperature
3 cloves garlic, crushed
1½ cups home-cooked cannellini beans, or 1 (15-ounce) can, drained and rinsed
1 tablespoon balsamic vinegar
1 teaspoon chopped fresh oregano, or ½ teaspoon dried
¼ cup plus 2 tablespoons chopped fresh basil

2 tablespoons water
Salt and freshly ground black pepper
1 fresh plum tomato, sliced paper thin
½ cup chopped roasted red bell peppers, jarred or homemade (see page 16)
1 (6-ounce) jar marinated artichoke hearts, drained and sliced
½ cup pitted kalamata olives, coarsely chopped
⅓ cup sliced marinated mushrooms

Position the oven rack on the lowest level of the oven, and preheat the oven to 425°F.

Spread the crust onto a pizza pan, stretching to fit. Set aside.

In a food processor, combine the garlic, beans, vinegar, oregano, the 2 tablespoons basil, the water, and salt and pepper to taste. Process until smooth. Spread the mixture

evenly onto the pizza crust, to within ½ inch of the edge. Arrange the tomato, peppers, artichokes, olives, and mushrooms on top of the pizza, spacing them aesthetically. Bake until the crust is golden brown, about 15 minutes.

Serve hot, sprinkled with the remaining ¼ cup basil.

snowballs in hell

serves 4

baking time: 30 minutes

These tasty "snowballs," made with white beans, garlic, and tofu, are absolutely delicious cloaked in a fiery "hell" sauce. Don't let the playful title fool you—this recipe is one serious flavor sensation. Or, I should say, three flavor sensations, since I provide variations for three kinds of hell sauce: one prepared arrabiata style; with hot red pepper and cayenne; one made with chipotles; and another based on sriracha.

3 cloves garlic, minced
1½ cups home-cooked white beans, or
   1 (15-ounce) can, drained and rinsed
1 cup extra-firm tofu, drained
½ teaspoon salt
2 tablespoons olive oil, plus more for
   cooking balls

½ cup bread crumbs
¼ cup vital wheat gluten flour
½ teaspoon dried oregano
¼ teaspoon dried thyme
¼ teaspoon dried basil

Preheat the oven to 375°F. Oil a shallow baking dish. Combine the garlic, beans, tofu, salt, the 2 tablespoons oil, the bread crumbs, vital wheat gluten flour, oregano, thyme, and basil in a food processor, pulsing to blend. Shape into 1½-inch balls and arrange in the prepared shallow baking dish. Drizzle with additional oil and bake for 30 minutes, turning once.

To serve, make one of the sauces below while the snowballs bake. Spoon the sauce around the balls, and serve hot.

hell sauce arrabiata style

1 tablespoon olive oil
5 cloves garlic, finely minced
1 (28-ounce) can crushed tomatoes
1 teaspoon red pepper flakes
1 teaspoon sugar
1 teaspoon salt
½ teaspoon dried oregano
½ teaspoon dried basil
¼ teaspoon cayenne
¼ teaspoon freshly ground black pepper

Heat the oil in a saucepan over medium heat. Add the garlic and cook until fragrant, 1 minute. Stir in the tomatoes, red pepper flakes, sugar, salt, oregano, basil, cayenne, and pepper. Simmer until the flavors are well blended, 10 to 15 minutes.

hell sauce chipotle style

1 tablespoon olive oil
5 cloves garlic, finely minced
1 (28-ounce) can crushed tomatoes
1 teaspoon red pepper flakes
1 teaspoon sugar
1 teaspoon salt
4 to 5 chipotle chiles in adobo, pureed or
   finely minced

Heat the oil in a saucepan over medium heat. Add the garlic and cook until fragrant, 1 minute. Stir in the tomatoes, red pepper flakes, sugar, salt, and chiles. Simmer until the flavors are well blended, 10 to 15 minutes.

hell sauce sriracha style

1 tablespoon olive oil
5 cloves garlic, finely minced
1 (28-ounce) can crushed tomatoes
1 teaspoon red pepper flakes
1 teaspoon sugar
1 teaspoon salt
1 tablespoon sriracha sauce or other
   Asian chili sauce

Heat the oil in a saucepan over medium heat. Add the garlic and cook until fragrant, 1 minute. Stir in the tomatoes, red pepper flakes, sugar, salt, and sriracha. Simmer until the flavors are well blended, 10 to 15 minutes.

sauces
and
condiments

Sometimes all it takes is a good sauce or condiment to transform a meal from simple to sensational. That's what this chapter is all about.

Let recipes like Spicy Tomato Achar, Hoisin-Peanut Sauce, or Lemon-Cashew Cream Sauce perk up tofu, tempeh, or noodles. Turn sautéed seitan into a savory main dish with Sienna Sauce or Country Gravy with Bits of Onion. Both of these brown sauces are also great over mashed potatoes or cooked grains. The Three-Nut Cheeze Whiz is a real whiz in the kitchen—use it on nachos, over roasted or steamed vegetables, or tossed with pasta.

If you're looking for a great marinade for vegetables, tempeh, tofu, or seitan, try the Hoisin-Miso Marinade. Rounding out the chapter is a luscious fruit chutney, two kinds of dipping sauces, and the versatile Mix-and-Match Pesto. When it comes to sauces and condiments, this chapter has it all.

sienna sauce

makes about 2½ cups

This is my go-to brown sauce that has a rich depth of flavor and a lovely warm sienna color. Add sliced mushrooms and a splash of wine (red, white, or fortified) to suit your needs. It is used to make the sauces for Seitan Forestière (see page 162) and Tempeh with Mellow Mustard Sauce (see page 163) but is also delicious on its own over sautéed seitan, mashed potatoes, cooked grains, or roasted vegetables.

2 tablespoons olive oil
½ cup minced yellow onion
½ cup minced carrots
2 cloves garlic, minced
¼ cup all-purpose flour
2 cups vegetable broth
2 tablespoons soy sauce

2 teaspoons tomato paste
1 teaspoon minced fresh marjoram, or
    ½ teaspoon dried
1 teaspoon minced fresh thyme, or
    ½ teaspoon dried
1 teaspoon browning sauce (Kitchen
    Bouquet and Gravy Master are vegan)

In a large saucepan, heat the oil over medium heat. Add the onion, carrots, and garlic. Cook, stirring, until softened, about 5 minutes. Add the flour and stir constantly until it is absorbed, about 1 minute. Slowly stir in 1 cup of the broth. When the mixture thickens, stir in the remaining 1 cup broth, the soy sauce, tomato paste, marjoram, and thyme. Stir until the mixture becomes smooth. Simmer over low heat until the flavors are well blended, 5 to 7 minutes. Stir in the browning sauce.

Puree the sauce in the saucepan with an immersion blender, or in a stand blender or food processor and return to the pot. Serve hot. If not using right away, cool the sauce to room temperature, transfer to a container, cover, and refrigerate until needed. Properly stored, the sauce will keep for about 3 days.

country gravy with bits of onion

makes about 1¾ cups

This is an easy herb-laced gravy that can be used to top everything from mashed potatoes and seitan to veggie burgers or baked grain and bean loaves. If you're not a fan of the tiny onion pieces, simply puree the gravy for a smooth sauce.

2 tablespoons olive oil
½ cup minced onion
2 tablespoons all-purpose flour
1 tablespoon soy sauce
1 teaspoon dried thyme

½ teaspoon dried sage
⅓ teaspoon salt
¼ teaspoon freshly ground black pepper
1 cup vegetable broth
½ cup unflavored soy creamer

Heat the oil in a saucepan over medium heat. Add the onion and cook until softened, 3 minutes. Sprinkle on the flour and stir to mix. Add the soy sauce, thyme, sage, salt, and pepper, and stir to combine. Pour in the broth, stirring until it thickens and becomes smooth, about 5 minutes. Reduce the heat to low, and stir in the soy creamer. Taste and adjust the seasonings. For a smoother texture, puree the gravy in a blender or food processor. Serve hot. Store any unused sauce in the refrigerator in a tightly covered container.

better than béchamel

makes about 2 cups

This all-purpose white sauce can be used to top vegetable patties or croquettes, as a sauce for pasta, or as a binder for casseroles. For a richer, thicker sauce, add ¼ cup vegan cream cheese and process until well blended.

3 tablespoons vegan butter (Earth Balance)
½ cup minced shallot
1 clove garlic, minced
3 tablespoons all-purpose flour
2 tablespoons dry white wine
1 cup vegetable broth

1 cup unsweetened soy creamer or thick
   unsweetened nondairy milk, such as
   MimicCreme (see note)
Dash of ground nutmeg
Salt and freshly ground white pepper

In a saucepan, heat the vegan butter over medium heat. Add the shallot and garlic and cook until softened, about 3 minutes. Do not brown. Stir in the flour and cook, stirring, until it is absorbed, about 1 minute. Stir in the wine, broth, soy creamer, nutmeg, and salt and white pepper to taste. Cook, stirring, until thickened, 3 to 5 minutes. Transfer the sauce to a blender or food processor and blend until smooth, then return to the saucepan and heat over low heat until hot. Serve immediately. If not using right away, transfer to a container and set aside until cool, then cover and refrigerate until needed. Properly stored, the sauce will keep for up to 3 days.

note: Instead of a vegan creamer or milk, use cashew cream, made by combining about ¾ cup raw cashews (soaked overnight) in a blender with enough water to cover by 1-inch and blending until smooth.

lemon-cashew cream sauce

makes about 2 cups

This sauce is so good you may be tempted to drink it. Use it as a luscious topping for roasted vegetables, cooked grains, bean patties, and a host of other dishes, including my favorite way to enjoy it—tossed with cooked pasta and vegetables.

½ cup raw cashews
3 tablespoons nutritional yeast
1 cup unsweetened nondairy milk
¾ cup vegetable broth
1 teaspoon salt

⅛ teaspoon ground cayenne
2 tablespoons freshly squeezed lemon juice
1 teaspoon mellow white miso paste
  (optional)

In a high-speed blender or food processor (see note), process the cashews to a fine powder. Add the nutritional yeast and nondairy milk and blend until smooth. Transfer to a saucepan and add the broth, salt, and cayenne. Heat over medium heat, stirring until hot and slightly thickened, about 7 minutes. Stir in the lemon juice and miso, if using. Serve hot. If not using right away, transfer to a container and set aside to cool, then cover and refrigerate until needed. Properly stored, it will keep for 3 days.

note: If not using a high-speed blender, soak the cashews overnight to soften, then drain well and make the sauce in a food processor.

three-nut cheeze whiz

makes about 2 cups

Cashews, tahini, and almond milk get whizzed together in a blender to make a thick and creamy sauce with a cheesy flavor. Use it to make vegan mac and cheese or in other casseroles where a cheesy flavor is desired. It's also great drizzled over chili or pasta, or to make nachos. If you don't have a high-speed blender, soak the cashews in water overnight to soften for a smoother texture.

⅔ cup raw cashews (see headnote)
⅓ cup nutritional yeast
1 teaspoon salt
1 clove garlic, crushed
2 tablespoons tahini

1 cup unsweetened almond milk, or more
   if needed
1 tablespoon freshly squeezed lemon juice
1 teaspoon cider vinegar
½ teaspoon prepared yellow mustard

In a high-speed blender, combine the cashews, nutritional yeast, and salt, and grind to a powder. Add the garlic, tahini, the 1 cup almond milk, the lemon juice, vinegar, and mustard and blend until smooth and creamy. Use as is or transfer to a saucepan and heat over low heat until hot, adding more almond milk if the sauce is too thick. If not using right away, transfer to a container and cover and refrigerate until needed. Properly stored, the sauce will keep for up to 3 days.

hoisin–peanut sauce

makes about 1½ cups

It seems like there are dozens of ways to make peanut sauce, and here's one more. What sets this apart is the addition of hoisin, adding its richly aromatic flavor to the sauce. Serve this with fried or baked spring rolls, or chunks of fried or baked tofu. You can also toss it with cooked noodles and vegetables.

⅓ cup creamy peanut butter
¼ cup hoisin sauce
¼ cup soy sauce
2 tablespoons rice vinegar
1 tablespoon sesame oil
1 tablespoon sriracha sauce

2 teaspoons grated fresh ginger
2 teaspoons agave nectar, or 1 teaspoon
  sugar
1 tablespoon minced scallions
2 teaspoons toasted sesame seeds
½ cup hot water

Combine all the ingredients in a small bowl and stir until well blended. The sauce is now ready to use. If not using right away, cover and refrigerate until needed. Properly stored, the sauce will keep for up to 3 days.

spicy tomato achar

makes about 1½ cups

Achar is a spicy Nepali sauce that is a must-have condiment with momo dumplings, but it's also delicious spooned over rice or grilled tofu. It's even good as a dip for tortilla chips or pita chips. If you prefer a less spicy sauce, use only one chile instead of two.

1 (14-ounce) can fire-roasted or regular diced tomatoes, well drained
1 cup coarsely chopped fresh cilantro
2 hot chiles, seeded and chopped
2 cloves garlic, crushed
1 tablespoon grated fresh ginger

2 teaspoons freshly squeezed lemon juice
½ teaspoon ground cumin
½ teaspoon curry powder
½ teaspoon smoked paprika
½ teaspoon sugar
½ teaspoon salt

In a blender or food processor, combine the tomatoes, cilantro, chiles, garlic, ginger, lemon juice, cumin, curry powder, paprika, sugar, and salt. Blend until smooth. Transfer to a bowl. If not using right away, cover and refrigerate until needed. Properly stored, the sauce will keep for 3 to 4 days.

variation: Stir in 1 tablespoon tahini and sprinkle with toasted sesame seeds.

tomatillo–cilantro salsa

makes about 2 cups

For a flavorful change from the usual tomato salsa, try this salsa verde made with tomatillos and cilantro. Serrano or jalapeño chiles add heat—use 1 or 2 depending on how much heat you like.

2 teaspoons olive oil
¼ cup chopped yellow onion
2 cloves garlic, minced
8 to 10 tomatillos, chopped (about 2 cups)

1 to 2 serrano or jalapeño chiles, seeded and chopped
½ cup lightly packed fresh cilantro, coarsely chopped
½ teaspoon salt

Heat the oil in a saucepan over medium heat. Add the onion, garlic, tomatillos, and chile and cook to mellow the flavors, 5 minutes. Transfer the tomatillo mixture to a food processor. Add the cilantro and salt and pulse until finely minced.

Transfer to a bowl and set aside to cool to room temperature. If not using right away, cover and refrigerate until needed. Properly stored, the sauce will keep for up to 3 days.

hoisin–miso marinade

makes about ¾ cup

The combination of miso paste and hoisin sauce give this easy marinade a rich depth of flavor with a touch of heat from the sriracha. Use it to marinate tofu, tempeh, or portobello mushrooms for 3 to 6 hours or overnight. The leftover marinade can then be simmered until hot and used as a cooking sauce over whatever was marinated in it. For a thicker sauce, when simmering, stir in 1 to 2 teaspoons of cornstarch that have been dissolved in 1 to 2 tablespoons of water.

¼ cup hoisin sauce
2 tablespoons white miso paste
2 tablespoons soy sauce
2 tablespoons rice vinegar
2 tablespoons water

1 tablespoon toasted sesame oil
1 tablespoon minced fresh garlic
2 scallions, minced
1 teaspoon grated fresh ginger
1 teaspoon sriracha sauce

Combine all the ingredients in a small bowl, stirring to blend. The marinade is now ready to use. If not using right away, cover and refrigerate until needed. Properly stored, the sauce will keep for up to 4 days.

cranberry cumberland sauce

makes about 1½ cups

Cranberries provide a new twist on the classic Cumberland sauce, traditionally made with currant jelly. If you're a fan of sweet-savory sauces, try this with sautéed seitan or tempeh.

¼ cup port wine
¼ cup minced shallots
1 cup whole-berry cranberry sauce, canned or homemade
1 tablespoon grated lemon zest
2 teaspoons grated fresh ginger

1 tablespoon Dijon mustard
1½ tablespoons freshly squeezed lemon juice
½ teaspoon salt
¼ teaspoon freshly ground black pepper

Combine the port and shallots in a saucepan and bring to a simmer. Add the cranberry sauce and cook, stirring, over low heat to combine, about 5 minutes. Add the lemon zest, ginger, mustard, lemon juice, salt, and pepper, and simmer until the flavors are well blended, 5 minutes. Serve hot. If not using right away, transfer to a container and set aside until cool, then cover and refrigerate until needed. Properly stored, the sauce will keep for up to 3 days.

golden pineapple–raisin chutney

makes about 2½ cups

Making your own chutney is so simple, and it's a great way to save money since store-bought chutney can cost big bucks. Pineapple and golden raisins are one of my favorite combinations, but you can use other ingredients, such as mango, to suit your own tastes and what you have on hand.

2 cups chopped pineapple, fresh or
   drained canned
½ cup golden raisins
¼ cup minced red onion
1½ tablespoons cider vinegar

1 tablespoon packed light brown sugar
2 teaspoons grated fresh ginger
½ teaspoon red pepper flakes
⅛ teaspoon salt

Combine all the ingredients in a saucepan over medium-high heat and cook, stirring, until hot and well mixed, 5 minutes. Once the mixture is hot, reduce the heat to low and simmer over medium heat, stirring frequently, until the ingredients have softened and begin to meld, 12 to 14 minutes. Transfer to a bowl and cool to room temperature. Taste and adjust the seasonings. Serve at room temperature or chilled. If not using right away, transfer to a container and set aside until cool, then cover and refrigerate until needed. Properly stored, the sauce will keep for up to 5 days.

mix-and-match pesto

makes about 1 cup

Customize your own signature pesto with your choice of ingredient options. Use more or less garlic, according to taste; include nutritional yeast for a cheesier flavor; add some red pepper flakes for a little heat; go with an all basil pesto, or add another herb or another ingredient; choose a different nut to add to a unique flavor profile. The end result might be: cilantro-cashew pesto; mint-macadamia pesto; or spinach-walnut pesto—you decide. For extra flavor, used lightly toasted nuts.

3 to 5 cloves garlic
½ teaspoon salt
1 teaspoon white miso paste
1 tablespoon nutritional yeast (optional)
**¼ to ½ teaspoon red pepper flakes
    (optional)**
1 cup packed fresh basil leaves

**½ cup fresh cilantro, parsley, or mint;
    spinach; or oil-packed sun-dried
    tomatoes**
**⅓ cup cashews, macadamia nuts, walnuts,
    or pine nuts**
⅓ cup olive oil

In a food processor, combine the garlic, salt, miso, nutritional yeast, if using, and red pepper flakes, and process to a paste. Add the basil, cilantro (or other ingredient), and nuts and process to a paste. With the machine running, add the oil until well blended. If not using right away, transfer to a tightly covered container and refrigerate until needed. Properly stored, the pesto will keep for up to 3 days.

oil-free mango dipping sauce

makes about ¾ cup

Pureed mango contributes flavor and body to this tasty oil-free sauce. It's ideal as a dipping sauce for fresh spring rolls or baked tofu chunks. It also makes a delicious salad dressing. For a spicy version, add a dash of red pepper flakes or sriracha sauce.

⅔ cup diced fresh mango
2 tablespoons rice vinegar
2 tablespoons mango or apple juice
2 teaspoons chopped fresh parsley or
  cilantro

1 teaspoon chopped shallots
⅛ teaspoon salt
Pinch of freshly ground black pepper
⅛ teaspoon sugar, or ½ teaspoon maple
  syrup or agave nectar

Combine all the ingredients in a blender and blend until smooth. Taste and adjust the seasonings. Serve immediately, or transfer to a small bowl and cover and refrigerate until needed. This sauce is best if used on the same day that it is made.

sesame–ponzu dipping sauce

makes about ½ cup

Fragrant with citrus and sesame, this flavorful sauce is an ideal dipping sauce to serve with baked or fried spring rolls, gyoza, or vegetable tempura. It's also good drizzled over baked tofu.

3 tablespoons soy sauce
2 tablespoons ponzu sauce
2 tablespoons orange juice
1 tablespoon tahini
2 teaspoons toasted sesame oil

1 scallion, minced
2 teaspoons sesame seeds
1 teaspoon grated fresh ginger
½ teaspoon sugar
½ teaspoon red pepper flakes (optional)

In a small bowl, combine all the ingredients and mix well. Use immediately or cover and refrigerate until needed. Properly stored, this sauce will keep for up to 3 days.

(almost) effortless desserts

Homemade desserts often conjure thoughts of time-consuming made-from-scratch cakes or temperamental pie crusts. But it doesn't have to be that way thanks to this collection of easy-to-prepare dessert recipes. From after-school treats such as Cranberry–Almond Oat Bars or Harvest Cookies, to luscious Tiramisu Parfaits and Catalan-Style Crème Brûlée, both fancy enough to serve company, these desserts will satisfy any sweet tooth.

The chapter contains several yummy cookie recipes such as Coconut Pistachio Cookies, Butterscotch Apple Cookies, and Molasses Ginger Cookies with Blueberries. You will also find flaky pastry desserts including Pear Turnovers, Banana Split en Croûte, and the amazing Shortcut Baklava made with puff pastry instead of phyllo. There's also a "cake" made entirely of ripe seasonal fruit, and decadent and delicious Ginger–Cashew Chocolate Truffles. Can you really make desserts like these in 30 minutes? Yes, you can.

NOTE: The vegan butter used in these recipes is Earth Balance brand buttery spread.

butterscotch apple cookies

makes about 2½ dozen

Bits of apple and butterscotch chips make these moist round cookies a favorite in our house. Dusted with confectioners' sugar, they're not too sweet and make a terrific accompaniment to a cup of hot tea or coffee. Vegan butterscotch chips are available online and in some supermarkets (the Food Lion store brand is vegan).

½ cup vegan butter
¼ cup applesauce
1 tablespoon maple syrup
⅓ cup confectioners' sugar, plus more for dusting
1 teaspoon vanilla extract

1 teaspoon ground cinnamon
¼ teaspoon salt
1½ cups all-purpose flour
½ cup vegan butterscotch chips
½ cup shredded or finely chopped apple

Preheat the oven to 375°F. In a bowl, combine the vegan butter, applesauce, maple syrup, the ⅓ cup confectioners' sugar, the vanilla, cinnamon, and salt and beat until creamy and well blended. Gradually beat in the flour, then stir in the butterscotch chips and apple pieces. Use a tablespoon to scoop the dough and shape into 1-inch balls. Arrange on an ungreased baking sheet.

Bake until golden brown, 10 to 12 minutes. While they are still hot, sift a dusting of confectioners' sugar onto the cookies. Transfer to a cooling rack to cool completely.

harvest cookies

makes about 2 dozen

Lots of fruit, nuts, oats, and spices make these wholesome and delicious cookies ideal for fall and winter baking when their fragrance fills the house and makes you feel warm inside.

⅓ cup vegan butter, at room temperature
½ cup light brown sugar
¼ cup granulated sugar
¼ cup maple syrup
¼ cup applesauce
1 teaspoon vanilla extract
1 cup all-purpose flour
½ teaspoon baking powder
1 teaspoon ground cinnamon

½ teaspoon ground allspice
½ teaspoon ground ginger
¼ teaspoon salt
1¼ cups quick-cooking oats
¼ cup chopped walnuts
¼ cup dried cranberries
¼ cup golden raisins or chopped dried apples

Preheat the oven to 350°F. Combine the vegan butter, brown sugar, and granulated sugar in a bowl and cream them together until smooth. Add the maple syrup, applesauce, and vanilla, and mix well to combine.

In a separate bowl, combine the flour, baking powder, cinnamon, allspice, ginger, and salt. Add the flour mixture to the butter mixture. Stir in the oats, walnuts, cranberries, and raisins, and mix well to combine. Drop by the tablespoonful onto a cookie sheet and flatten the tops a little with a spatula. Bake until nicely browned, about 15 minutes. Transfer to a rack to cool.

molasses ginger cookies with blueberries

makes about 2½ dozen

The combination of ginger and blueberries makes these cookies stand out from the crowd. With a soft texture and a flavor reminiscent of gingerbread (but with blueberries!), they taste best after they've had a chance to cool.

⅓ cup vegan butter, at room temperature
½ cup molasses
⅓ cup maple syrup
¼ cup applesauce
1 teaspoon vanilla extract
2¼ cups all-purpose flour
1 teaspoon baking powder

½ teaspoon baking soda
1¼ teaspoons ground ginger
½ teaspoon ground cinnamon
½ teaspoon salt
1 cup fresh or frozen blueberries

Preheat the oven to 375°F. Lightly grease a cookie sheet and set aside.

In a bowl, combine the vegan butter, molasses, maple syrup, applesauce, and vanilla and cream together until well mixed.

In a separate bowl, combine the flour, baking powder, baking soda, ginger, cinnamon, and salt. Mix well, then add the flour mixture to the butter mixture. Add the blueberries and stir to mix well. Pinch off the dough into 1-inch balls and arrange on the prepared cookie sheet. Flatten with a metal spatula and bake until browned, 12 minutes. Allow to cool completely on a cooling rack before serving.

tip: Because the dough is especially sticky, when pressing the cookies down, spray nonstick spray on the back of the metal spatula to help prevent them from sticking to the spatula.

coconut pistachio cookies

makes about 2 dozen

I love the elegant look of these white cookies with flecks of green pistachio. And their taste is sublime. You can cut them in any shape you want, or simply roll the dough into a rectangle and use a pastry cutter to cut squares—quick, easy, and best of all, no waste.

1 cup sugar
½ cup vegan cream cheese, at room
  temperature
½ cup vegan butter, at room temperature

2 cups all-purpose flour
1 teaspoon baking powder
⅓ cup chopped pistachios
⅓ cup flaked coconut

Preheat the oven to 375°F. Line 2 cookie sheets with parchment paper and set aside. In a food processor, combine the sugar, cream cheese, and vegan butter, and process until smooth and well blended. Add the flour and baking powder, and process until well combined. Transfer to a bowl and stir in the pistachios and coconut. Mix well, then transfer the cookie dough to a flat work surface between two sheets of plastic wrap. Roll out to ½ inch thick. Use a cookie cutter, pastry cutter, or small drinking glass to cut out the cookies and arrange them on the cookie sheets. Bake until golden, about 15 minutes. Transfer to a cooking rack to cool completely before serving.

crispy chocolate trail mix squares

makes 9 squares

Cocoa adds a chocolaty nuance to these tasty squares made with a variety of fruits, nuts, and seeds—the result of wanting a healthier alternative to those nostalgic cereal squares we grew up with.

¼ cup slivered almonds
¼ cup sunflower seeds
1½ cups crispy rice cereal
½ cup semisweet vegan chocolate chips
¼ cup dried cranberries
¼ cup dried shredded coconut
2 tablespoons unsweetened cocoa
1 tablespoon all-purpose flour

1 ripe banana, cut into chunks
⅓ cup agave nectar or maple syrup
¼ cup almond butter
1 tablespoon vegan butter, at room temperature
1 teaspoon vanilla extract
1 teaspoon freshly squeezed lemon juice
½ teaspoon baking powder

Preheat the oven to 400°F. Grease a 9-inch square baking pan and set aside.

Pulse the almonds and sunflower seeds in a food processor until finely ground and transfer to a bowl. Add the cereal, chocolate chips, cranberries, coconut, cocoa, and flour. Mix well and transfer to a bowl.

In the food processor, combine the banana, agave, almond butter, vegan butter, vanilla, lemon juice, and baking powder, and process until smooth and well blended. Add the banana mixture to the fruits, nuts, and seeds mixture and stir to mix well.

Press the mixture into the prepared pan and bake until firm and nicely browned, 25 minutes. Allow to cool for a few minutes before cutting into squares.

chocolate cheesecake squares

makes 9 squares

The decadently delicious flavor of chocolate cheesecake takes a casual turn when baked in a pan and cut into squares. Garnish with your choice of fresh berries, toasted nuts, or chocolate curls, or do as Lea Jacobson did when she tested this recipe: top the squares with broken pretzel pieces and a drizzle of balsamic glaze.

1½ cups vegan chocolate cookie crumbs
2 tablespoons light brown sugar
¼ cup vegan butter, melted
2 (8-ounce) containers vegan cream
   cheese, at room temperature
¾ cup granulated sugar

⅔ cup vegan semisweet chocolate chips,
   melted
1 teaspoon pure vanilla extract
Chopped nuts, fresh berries, or chocolate
   curls, for garnish

Preheat the oven to 350°F. Grease an 8-inch square baking pan and set aside. In a bowl, combine the cookie crumbs, brown sugar, and vegan butter and mix to moisten the crumbs. Press the crumb mixture into the prepared baking pan and bake until lightly toasted, 5 minutes. Set aside.

In a food processor, combine the cream cheese, sugar, chocolate, and vanilla and process until smooth. Spread the mixture onto the crust. Bake until firm, 20 minutes. Cool to room temperature, then refrigerate until chilled. To serve, cut into squares and garnish with the chopped nuts, berries, or chocolate curls.

cranberry–almond oat bars

makes 15 to 16 bars

These no-bake bars are made with wholesome pantry ingredients including granola, quick oats, almonds, and dried cranberries. They can be assembled in a flash and make a great after-school snack for the kids (or an anytime treat for you).

2½ cups quick oats
½ cup granola
½ cup dried cranberries
½ cup sliced or slivered almonds
Pinch of salt

1¼ cups almond butter
⅔ cup agave nectar or maple syrup
1 tablespoon vegan butter
1 teaspoon vanilla extract

Grease an 8-inch square baking pan and set aside. In a large bowl, combine the oats, granola, cranberries, almonds, and salt. Mix well and set aside.

In a saucepan over medium heat, combine the almond butter, agave, and vegan butter, and stir until smooth and well blended. Remove from the heat, stir in the vanilla, then add to the dry mixture in the bowl. Mix until well combined.

Press the mixture into the prepared baking pan. Refrigerate until chilled, then cut into bars, approximately 1 by 3 inches.

shortcut baklava

serves 6

Puff pastry instead of phyllo dough is the key to this nontraditional baklava for a quick-fix way to enjoy the flavors of baklava without all the fuss. Either walnuts or pistachios are found in traditional baklava, so use whichever you prefer. Some classic versions don't include spices, but I like the addition of cinnamon and a touch of ginger.

1½ cups coarsely ground walnuts or pistachios
¼ cup granulated sugar
¼ cup agave nectar
2 tablespoons vegan butter, melted

1¼ teaspoons ground cinnamon
¼ teaspoon ground ginger
1 teaspoon pure vanilla extract
1 sheet frozen vegan puff pastry, thawed
Confectioners' sugar

Preheat the oven to 400°F. Line a baking sheet with parchment paper or a silicone baking mat and set aside. In a medium bowl, combine the walnuts, granulated sugar, agave, vegan butter, cinnamon, ginger, and vanilla and mix well to combine. Set aside.

Unroll the puff pastry onto a lightly floured work surface. Roll out the pastry to a thin rectangle, about 10 by 12 inches, then cut in half lengthwise. Arrange one piece of the pastry on the prepared baking sheet. Sprinkle the nut mixture evenly over the pastry. Top

with the remaining pastry and pinch the edges together to seal the filling inside. You should have a filled pastry rectangle about 5 by 12 inches. Prick the top of the pastry with a fork and sprinkle the top of the pastry with a light dusting of confectioners' sugar.

Bake until golden, about 18 minutes, then use a metal spatula to gently slide the baklava onto a cooling rack to cool. When ready to serve, transfer to a cutting board and cut into slices. Serve warm.

pear turnovers

serves 4

I prefer the flavor of Bosc pears, but you can use Anjou or Bartlett, if you prefer. One 7 to 8-ounce pear is enough for four turnovers. If your pears are on the small side, you may need two. The recipe is easily doubled, or you could make smaller turnovers by cutting the pastry into smaller squares.

1 large ripe pear (or 2 medium), cored and finely chopped
¼ cup chopped toasted walnuts (see page 17) (optional)
¼ cup golden raisins (optional)
2 tablespoons light brown sugar

1 teaspoon cornstarch
1 teaspoon ground cinnamon
⅛ teaspoon ground cloves
1 sheet frozen vegan puff pastry, thawed
Confectioners' sugar, for serving

Preheat the oven to 400°F. In a bowl, combine the pear, walnuts, if using, raisins, if using, brown sugar, cornstarch, cinnamon, and cloves. Mix well to combine. Set aside.

Roll out the pastry on a lightly floured work surface and cut into four equal pieces.

Spoon the filling mixture evenly onto each dough piece, then fold one end of the dough over the filling to meet the opposite end of the dough. Use your fingers to seal and pinch the edges to enclose the filling.

Pierce the top of the pastry with a fork and arrange the turnovers on an ungreased baking sheet. Bake until golden brown, about 25 minutes. Transfer to a cooling rack to cool. When ready to serve, dust the tops lightly with confectioners' sugar.

banana split en croûte

serves 4

All the flavors of a banana split are baked into this flaky dessert. If you have vegan marshmallows, you can use them instead of the cream cheese mixture. For a delicious presentation, nestle each pastry next to a scoop of vegan ice cream and drizzle with chocolate syrup, nuts, and sliced strawberries.

2 ripe bananas
½ cup vegan cream cheese
2 tablespoons sugar
1 teaspoon vanilla extract
1 sheet frozen vegan puff pastry, thawed

¼ cup strawberry jam
½ cup semisweet chocolate chips
⅓ cup crushed unsalted peanuts
4 scoops vegan vanilla ice cream

Cut the ends off the bananas so they measure 4 to 5 inches in length, reserving the ends, then cut the bananas in half lengthwise and set aside.

In a food processor, combine the reserved banana ends with the cream cheese, sugar, and vanilla and process until smooth. Set aside. Preheat the oven to 400°F.

Roll out the pastry on a lightly floured work surface and divide into four equal pieces. Spread 1 tablespoon of the jam across each of the dough pieces. Spoon the cream cheese mixture evenly onto each piece of dough, then top each with a banana half, arranged across the longest width of the pastry. Sprinkle the bananas with chocolate chips and peanuts. Roll up the dough to enclose the filling, tucking in and pinching the ends so the filling remains inside. Pierce the top of the pastry with a fork and arrange the pastry logs on an ungreased baking sheet.

Bake until golden brown, about 20 minutes. To serve, cut each pastry in half diagonally and arrange on a dessert plate. Serve warm with a scoop of vegan vanilla ice cream.

stovetop fruit crisp

serves 4 to 6

This recipe is ideal for when you're short on time but in the mood for fresh-baked pie. It's so quick and easy—and you don't even need to turn on the oven. Best of all, it can be made with your choice of fresh or frozen fruit, so it can be enjoyed year-round. (In a pinch, you can even substitute canned pie filling in place of the fruit mixture.)

4 cups fresh or thawed and drained frozen
   sliced peaches
1 cup fresh or thawed frozen berries
⅓ to ½ cup granulated sugar
2 teaspoons freshly squeezed lemon juice
2 teaspoons cornstarch

1¼ cups granola
⅓ cup all-purpose flour
2 tablespoons light brown sugar
1 teaspoon ground cinnamon
½ teaspoon ground ginger
3 tablespoons neutral vegetable oil

In a 9-inch skillet, combine the peaches, berries, granulated sugar depending on the sweetness of the fruit, lemon juice, and cornstarch, stirring to coat the peaches. Set aside.

In a bowl, combine the granola, flour, brown sugar, cinnamon, ginger, and oil. Stir to combine, then spread the mixture evenly over the peaches. Cover and cook over medium heat until the peaches are tender and bubbly and the topping is cooked, 15 to 18 minutes. Uncover, remove from the heat, and allow to cool for 10 minutes before serving. Serve warm or at room temperature.

fresh-fruit cake

serves 6 to 8

This no-bake cake, made with a watermelon base decorated with berries and sliced fruit, is a fun way to serve fresh fruit in the summer. It makes a pretty presentation, and it's easy to assemble.

1 small round seedless watermelon
1 cup fresh blueberries or blackberries
1 cup fresh strawberries

1 kiwifruit, thinly sliced into rounds
1 star fruit, sliced (optional)

Place the watermelon on its side on a flat work surface and use a large knife to cut a slice off the stem end of the watermelon so that it sits flat on a work surface. Cut another slice off the opposite end of the watermelon so that you now have a flat bottom and top on the watermelon with the rind removed. Place a bowl with about the same diameter on top of the watermelon and use the edge of the bowl as a guide for your knife to cut away the rind from around the sides of the watermelon. You should be left with a pretty pink watermelon cake.

Transfer the watermelon cake to a large plate and decorate aesthetically on the top and around the bottom with the blueberries, strawberries, kiwifruit, and star fruit, if using. Cut into wedges to serve.

maple–pecan baked pears

serves 4

Use your favorite variety of pears to make this delicious and wholesome dessert. The chopped pecans and dates add wonderful flavor notes to the pears. Serve warm with a scoop of vegan vanilla ice cream.

4 ripe pears, halved lengthwise and cored
2 teaspoons freshly squeezed lemon juice
¼ cup finely chopped pecans
2 tablespoons chopped pitted dates

¼ cup pure maple syrup
¼ teaspoon ground cinnamon
¼ teaspoon ground ginger

Preheat the oven to 400°F. Oil a 10-inch square baking dish. Arrange the pear halves in the prepared baking dish, cut side up. Brush the cut surface of the pears with the lemon juice and set aside.

In a bowl, combine the pecans, dates, syrup, cinnamon, and ginger, stirring to mix well. Spoon the mixture into the pear halves, dividing evenly. Cover and bake until the pears are tender, about 20 minutes. To serve, scoop two pear halves each into 4 shallow dessert bowls. Serve warm.

tiramisu parfaits

serves 4

Tiramisu is one of my husband's favorite desserts, but I usually make it only for company because traditional tiramisu can be time consuming. That's why I came up with this no-fuss variation: all the luscious creamy coffee and chocolate flavor of tiramisu in a fraction of the time. If you don't have parfait glasses, martini or wine glasses are a good choice, but any dessert bowls will suffice.

½ cup hot black coffee
⅓ cup sugar
1 (8-ounce) container vegan cream cheese
⅓ cup cashew butter

1 teaspoon vanilla extract
8 to 12 vegan shortbread cookies
¼ cup Kahlúa or other coffee liqueur
Cocoa powder, for dusting

Combine the coffee and sugar in a small bowl, stirring to dissolve the sugar. Set aside to cool.

In a blender or food processor, combine the cream cheese, cashew butter, vanilla, and the reserved coffee mixture. Blend until smooth and creamy.

Break a cookie into the bottom of each of the 4 parfait glasses or other dessert glasses. Drizzle each with 1 teaspoon of Kahlúa and top with a spoonful of the cream cheese mixture. Repeat with the layering of the cookies, Kahlúa, and cream cheese mixture, until the glasses are full, ending with a layer of the cream cheese mixture, dusted with cocoa powder. Serve at once or refrigerate and serve chilled.

note: This dessert tastes best (and firms up a bit) if allowed to chill in the refrigerator for 1 to 2 hours, but it is also perfectly yummy if eaten right away.

apple pie parfaits

serves 4

Try these apple parfaits for the flavor of apple pie without all the work. Not only is this an easy and quick dessert, it's also very pretty when served in clear dessert glasses. If you don't have actual parfait glasses, wineglasses work well.

1 tablespoon vegan butter
2 Granny Smith apples, cored and thinly
   sliced
1 teaspoon freshly squeezed lemon juice
¼ cup light brown sugar
1½ teaspoons ground cinnamon
½ cup chopped toasted walnuts (see
   page 17)

¼ cup granola
1 cup silken tofu
⅓ cup almond butter
⅓ cup pure maple syrup
1 teaspoon vanilla extract

Heat the vegan butter in a skillet over medium heat. Add the apples, lemon juice, brown sugar, and 1 teaspoon of the cinnamon and cook, stirring, until the apples are softened, about 8 minutes. Transfer to a bowl and refrigerate to cool while you continue with the recipe.

In a separate bowl, combine the walnuts and granola and set aside.

In a blender or food processor, combine the tofu, almond butter, maple syrup, vanilla, and the remaining ½ teaspoon cinnamon. Blend until smooth and creamy.

Spoon a small amount of the walnut mixture into the bottom of 4 parfait glasses or other dessert glasses. Top with a spoonful of the apple mixture, followed by a spoonful of the tofu mixture. Repeat with the layering until the glasses are full, ending with a sprinkling of the walnut mixture. Serve at once or refrigerate and serve chilled.

note: Some apple varieties release a lot of juice when cooked, so be sure to drain off any excess liquid before spooning the cooked apples into the glasses.

catalan-style crème brûlée

serves 4

Catalan crème brûlée is made with lemon or orange. A vegan crème brûlée is made dairy-free, of course. This one is both. Serve warm or chilled. Vegan butterscotch chips are available online and in some supermarkets (the Food Lion store brand is vegan).

1 (12-ounce) package firm silken tofu, drained
2 ounces vegan cream cheese
¼ cup vegan butterscotch chips, melted
¼ cup vegan white chocolate chips, melted

½ cup sugar
¼ teaspoon vanilla extract
1 teaspoon lemon extract
2 tablespoons finely grated lemon zest

Preheat the oven to 375°F. Oil 4 ramekins or other ovenproof dessert dishes such as Pyrex custard cups. In a food processor or high-speed blender, combine the tofu, cream cheese, butterscotch chips, white chocolate chips, ¼ cup of the sugar, the vanilla, lemon extract, and lemon zest. Blend until very smooth and creamy.

Spoon the mixture equally into the prepared ramekins. Arrange the filled ramekins in a shallow baking dish. Carefully pour enough hot water into the baking dish to come halfway up the sides of the ramekins.

Bake until firm, about 20 minutes. Remove from the oven to cool for a few minutes. Set the oven to broil. Sprinkle each ramekin with the remaining sugar and transfer to a baking sheet. Place the ramekins under the broiler and broil until the sugar is browned. Alternately, a kitchen torch may be used to brown the sugar. Serve immediately, or cool to room temperature and refrigerate until chilled to serve cold.

note: For a smoother texture, you may need to add ½ teaspoon of neutral vegetable oil to the butterscotch and white chocolate chips when melting them.

ginger–cashew chocolate truffles

makes about 24 truffles

The creamy richness of cashews and the tantalizing bite of ginger team up with dates and cocoa to make decadent and sophisticated truffles. They're an elegant way to finish a meal and are also wonderful served with tea or coffee.

1 cup chopped pitted dates
1 cup unsalted cashews
⅓ cup cocoa powder, plus more for coating

2 tablespoons crystallized ginger
1 tablespoon cashew butter

Soak the dates in warm water until softened, about 10 minutes. Drain well and transfer to a food processor. Add the cashews, the ⅓ cup cocoa powder, the ginger, and cashew butter. Process until well combined. The mixture will appear crumbly, but try pinching off a little and shaping it into a ball before making any adjustments. If the mixture is too wet, add a bit more cocoa. If too dry, add a little more cashew butter or a teaspoon of water. Use your hands to roll the mixture into 1-inch balls, then roll them in additional cocoa to coat. Arrange on a plate and refrigerate to firm up. Keep refrigerated until ready to serve.

energy bites

makes about 24 pieces

Packed with protein, calcium, and other good things, these tasty treats make a great snack anytime you need a pick-me-up. Slightly sweet, these bites may be too wholesome to call dessert, so eat them whenever you want! (I've even been known to have a few for breakfast.)

½ cup unsalted cashews
½ cup walnuts or sunflower seeds
⅓ cup pitted dates
¼ cup tahini
2 tablespoons dried cranberries

1 tablespoon agave nectar or maple syrup
1½ teaspoons vanilla extract
Shredded coconut, finely ground nuts, or
  cocoa, for coating (optional)

Combine the cashews and walnuts in a food processor and process until finely ground. Add the dates, tahini, cranberries, agave, and vanilla and process until well combined. Pinch off a small amount of the mixture, roll into a 1-inch ball, and arrange on a cookie sheet. Repeat until all the mixture is used up. Roll the balls in coconut, nuts, or cocoa if desired. Refrigerate for 10 minutes to firm up or cover and refrigerate until ready to serve.

metric conversions and equivalents

metric conversion formulas

to convert	multiply
Ounces to grams	Ounces by 28.35
Pounds to kilograms	Pounds by .454
Teaspoons to milliliters	Teaspoons by 4.93
Tablespoons to milliliters	Tablespoons by 14.79
Fluid ounces to milliliters	Fluid ounces by 29.57
Cups to milliliters	Cups by 236.59
Cups to liters	Cups by .236
Pints to liters	Pints by .473
Quarts to liters	Quarts by .946
Gallons to liters	Gallons by 3.785
Inches to centimeters	Inches by 2.54

approximate metric equivalents

weight

¼ ounce	7 grams
½ ounce	14 grams
¾ ounce	21 grams
1 ounce	28 grams
1¼ ounces	35 grams
1½ ounces	42.5 grams
1⅔ ounces	45 grams
2 ounces	57 grams
3 ounces	85 grams
4 ounces (¼ pound)	113 grams
5 ounces	142 grams
6 ounces	170 grams
7 ounces	198 grams
8 ounces (½ pound)	227 grams
16 ounces (1 pound)	454 grams
35.25 ounces (2.2 pounds)	1 kilogram

volume

¼ teaspoon	1 milliliter
½ teaspoon	2.5 milliliters
¾ teaspoon	4 milliliters
1 teaspoon	5 milliliters
1¼ teaspoons	6 milliliters
1½ teaspoons	7.5 milliliters
1¾ teaspoons	8.5 milliliters
2 teaspoons	10 milliliters
1 tablespoon (½ fluid ounce)	15 milliliters
2 tablespoons (1 fluid ounce)	30 milliliters
¼ cup	60 milliliters
⅓ cup	80 milliliters
½ cup (4 fluid ounces)	120 milliliters
⅔ cup	160 milliliters
¾ cup	180 milliliters
1 cup (8 fluid ounces)	240 milliliters
1¼ cups	300 milliliters
1½ cups (12 fluid ounces)	360 milliliters
1⅔ cups	400 milliliters
2 cups (1 pint)	460 milliliters
3 cups	700 milliliters
4 cups (1 quart)	0.95 liter
1 quart plus ¼ cup	1 liter
4 quarts (1 gallon)	3.8 liters

length

⅛ inch	3 millimeters
¼ inch	6 millimeters
½ inch	1¼ centimeters
1 inch	2½ centimeters
2 inches	5 centimeters
2½ inches	6 centimeters
4 inches	10 centimeters
5 inches	13 centimeters
6 inches	15¼ centimeters
12 inches (1 foot)	30 centimeters

oven temperatures

To convert Fahrenheit to Celsius, subtract 32 from Fahrenheit, multiply the result by 5, then divide by 9.

description	fahrenheit	celsius	british gas mark
Very cool	200°	95°	0
Very cool	225°	110°	¼
Very cool	250°	120°	½
Cool	275°	135°	1
Cool	300°	150°	2
Warm	325°	165°	3
Moderate	350°	175°	4
Moderately hot	375°	190°	5
Fairly hot	400°	200°	6
Hot	425°	220°	7
Very hot	450°	230°	8
Very hot	475°	245°	9

common ingredients and their approximate equivalents

1 cup uncooked white rice = 185 grams
1 cup all-purpose flour = 140 grams
1 stick butter (4 ounces • ½ cup • 8 tablespoons) = 110 grams
1 cup butter (8 ounces • 2 sticks • 16 tablespoons) = 220 grams
1 cup brown sugar, firmly packed = 225 grams
1 cup granulated sugar = 200 grams

Information compiled from a variety of sources, including *Recipes into Type* by Joan Whitman and Dolores Simon (Newton, MA: Biscuit Books, 2000); *The New Food Lover's Companion* by Sharon Tyler Herbst (Hauppauge, NY: Barron's, 1995); and *Rosemary Brown's Big Kitchen Instruction Book* (Kansas City, MO: Andrews McMeel, 1998).

index